JAMINI ROY

A Painter Who Revisited the Roots

ANURADHA GHOSH

PAPER MISSILE
NIYOGI BOOKS

Published by
NIYOGI BOOKS
Block D, Building No. 77,
Okhla Industrial Area, Phase-I,
New Delhi-110 020, INDIA
Tel: 91-11-26816301, 26818960
Email: niyogibooks@gmail.com
Website: www.niyogibooksindia.com

Editor: Arkaprabha Biswas
Layout: Shashi Bhushan Prasad
Cover design: Anurag Hira
Cover illustrator: Douluri Narayana

ISBN: 978-93-91125-36-3
Publication: 2022

Publisher's note: Every effort has been made to ensure the accuracy of the information presented in this book. The images used in this book come from either the public domain or from the public commons, unless otherwise stated. The publisher welcomes comments and feedback from readers, in order to improve future editions, at niyogibooks@gmail.com.

Printed at Niyogi Offset Pvt. Ltd., New Delhi, India

For

Maya Majumder
Jogindranath Majumdar

CONTENTS

PRELUDE

As evening descends on the narrow, serpentine lanes of a North Calcutta neighbourhood, the artist scratches the paint off the canvas on which he had worked all day. Not once, but again and again, on successive days, with a palette knife that decidedly destroyed the painted image which continued to irk the artist with its inanity.

Something was amiss. He was painting only what he saw, but not what he felt. For it was, after all, only an exterior likeness; he had been looking instead for a visual approximation for the emotions and impulses which come about without shape and form. Exercises in mere eye-fooling exactness had ceased to speak to him, and he was in search of a new language in which he would find his voice.

This was Jamini Roy of the early 1920s, who had already made a name for himself for painting portraits.

He worked all day, relentlessly, on portraits in oils, commissioned works for which he had taken advance payment, and on which his livelihood depended. And then, as the day ended, he killed his own creation out of a deep dissatisfaction at the burden of senselessness he had to carry on with, in the name of a living, engaging in a brand of work he did not believe in any more. By then Roy was convinced that mere realism was inadequate to capture the essence of reality, for it was ultimately about the feeling mind, rooted both to emotion and the processing of experience. This act of repetitively inscribing and obliterating one's own creation stands as a powerful trope that adequately explains the very course of Jamini Roy's artistic career: he had to lose himself in order to find himself again.

LOCATING IDENTITY

Roy is usually remembered as one who drew his inspiration for his major body of works from the folk arts of Bengal, drawing from their simple placidity and a curious power to resist transformation brought about by a rapidly changing colonised society with its clear privileging of industrialisation and urbanisation. This, as a one-liner, would possibly serve its defining purpose, but only just: it would also be limiting our perspective on a painter who had created a singular, solitary path for himself and had walked it for the most part of his chequered career, and had succeeded in bringing about a decided change not only to Indian art, but also to the contemporary habits of art practice and collection.

And that is possibly the main problem in understanding Jamini Roy: his achievements are many-layered, connected often to areas beyond the strictly creative, that resist and repudiate such oversimplifications. Our understanding of and response to cultural history are curiously preferential to boxed categories—with labels—and this, more often than not, clearly defeats its own purpose. Images of Roy's major works had been a part of Bengal's visual culture for the longest time, and have a unique feature of identifiability even for the artistically disinclined public, something that can hardly be compared to anyone else's work. That is why a certain fixity of attitude about his paintings has imperceptibly developed among us. Now that we are several decades removed from the time when he lived and worked, it is vitally important for us to reappraise his career, identify the erasures and go beyond the popular line of appreciation that chiefly latches on only to the outer motifs and decorative features of his art.

It is difficult to understand the full significance of these transforming moments unless we refer to the variant nature of art practices during his own times, especially his early, formative years. Contemporary artistic practices both pulled and repelled him in his early years as a painter, and these contradictory tugs loosened the safe-seeming bait of a secure and settled livelihood and set him free to search after his own artistic identity. The art environment of his times was beset with a distinct polarity, with the contesting camps of the Orientalists, and the followers of Western academic naturalism. His early years saw the immense popularity of the works of the neo-Bengal school painters—Abanindranath Tagore himself, and his followers and disciples, often referred to as the 'Orientalists'—as opposed to the artists who painted in oils and followed Western realistic techniques. The Orientalists were trying to fashion an idiom of 'Indianness' in painting in line with the ideals of the Swadeshi movement of 1905, shunned both naturalism and oil painting, and in doing so, they turned for inspiration towards the ancient history, myths and traditions of an older, glorious India. They imagined, perhaps, that such reminiscences of glory would, in its turn, culminate in the resurgence of the nation wallowing in political and cultural captivity. There was, very much in place, a counterpoint to such ideals in the work of the 'academic' painters like Hemen Mazumdar, Atul Bose, B.C. Law and others who preferred to work in oils, favoured naturalism in art and opposed the revivalist tendencies of the former camp. Jamini Roy was close to this group at a time, and became notably proficient in naturalist techniques. Speaking about Roy's portraits, Atul Bose once said that he 'was the most able among those who painted in the Western Academic style in his time.'[1] Nevertheless, he is also known to have dabbled in the 'Indian' style for a while, and had also approached Abanindranath Tagore for inspiration. But it soon became clear that neither of these popular lines answered to his artistic quest. It was, rather, a space of unease that he had to contend with, a space that saw the rather confusing interface of what was Western and what was supposedly indigenous, complicated further by a plethora of contradictory discourses most of which attempted to define what the private journey of an artist should be all about. It was thus, finally, the question of identity that drove him to quietly turn away, not only from the trends of his time, but also from a livelihood provided by his frequently selling portraits. The living vitality of our villages, the inherent animation of their traditions and arts and their unassuming resistance to the upheavals introduced by both colonisation and industrialisation

---

1 Gupta, Radhaprasad. 1987. 'Jamini Royer Shilper Utso Sondhane'. *Desh*. p. 33.

spoke of an unbroken continuity of reassurance that appealed to him. It also engaged the confused aesthete in him who was yet to figure out the shape of national identity in art, and how it connected to the regional one.

For Roy, the village and its lifestyle, replete with the selfsame rhythms of the tranquil continuity of life, was not that conceptual illusive retreat, largely idealised, that had become a refuge of the weary urban creative artist of the world, who wanted to find wholeness in the seeming harmony of rurality away from their everyday experience of a fragmented life. There is a certain element of constructed unreality about such an idealisation, rather like the pastoral mode in literature, that involves a limited familiarity with the rural—something that does not apply for Jamini Roy at all. This idealisation, for him, was more of a return to his roots than the seeking of a distant, tranquil refuge. He belonged to a village himself—his approach was not that of a weary-hearted outsider who might make the mistake of over-reading. Instead, his intention was to revisit the strength and power of simplicity, the essence of life-affirming, unbroken traditions, with a mind that was already in tune with the modernist artistic innovations the world over.

Jamini Roy was born, according to known accounts, in mid-April of the year 1887, 'at midnight of the last day of the Bengali year',[2] to Ramtaran and Nagendrabala Roy, at Beliatore village, in the district of Bankura in West Bengal—a district famous for its exquisite terracotta toys, figurines, panels and the traditional *pats.*[3] His original name was Jamini Ranjan Roy—he dropped the middle name later in his life. From his very childhood, Roy was surrounded not only by this highly distinctive artistic and artisanal culture, but also by a very real experience of rural self-sufficiency. His father had opted for a farmer's life, having given up his government job and deciding to settle in the village, and grew different kinds of crops. He is also known to have taught drawing using his nails, instead of a pencil. Their family belonged to the upper

---

2 Dey, Bishnu. *Jamini Roy.* p. 18. This indicates that the date of Roy's birth may have been 14 April.

3 Traditionally, a *pat* is a rolled, painted scroll, usually slowly unrolled to an audience with an accompanying thread of narration, usually related to familiar religious or mythic tales. There were several regional varieties of *pats* in Bengal.

echelons of society,[4] especially his mother's side, but they willfully and happily merged with the agrarian livelihood and employed a number of cultivators and farm labourers who worked in the family-owned fields. Jamini, from his very childhood, came to understand that very real sense of self-sufficiency that works at the heart of a thriving village economy. Many years later, in an intimate reminiscence with his close friend Bishnu Dey, Roy recalls how even their clothes were spun by local weavers from the cotton his father grew. As they could not manage to weave red borders in sarees, his mother had to embroider slim borders with red threads before wearing these, as it was unthinkable then, for married women with living husbands, to wear sarees without borders! He also mentions how edible oil was processed from their own mustard crop, and oil from sesame was extracted

4 Roy's forefathers were connected with the royal family of Jessore. After the issuance of the death decree of the king, they fled to Mallabhum to seek refuge at the court of the king of Bishnupur. The King wished to gift them a *jagir* close to the royal palace as befitted their status, but they were wary of any closeness to royalty after their recent traumatic uprooting, and hence chose a forested tract of land at Beliatore, some distance away from Bishnupur. This was how the family's *zamindari* (landholding) was set up, at a remote, then-inaccessible location, skirted by forests that stretched from Manbhum to the district of Midnapore.

for use as hair oil.[5] The family also kept cattle, and his father often slept in the covered animal shed in order to protect them from the attack of wild animals which frequented the tracts of forests skirting the village. The young Jamini, who at times slept at nights alongside his father, was reassured by the fact that a cleaver was always kept ready by the bed to deal with intruding beasts. His father believed that whatever crops grew locally, in tune with not only the local climate but also the laws of nature, should actually be sufficient for people living in that area. This idea connects to the concept of limiting, abbreviating one's needs in order to be able to relate to the basic pattern of life: to identify, also, what is the essence and what is the excess, an attitude that gained prime importance in the mature line of work of the painter. This position was further mediated, and modified by Roy's close engagement with Western art movements many years

5 It is indeed interesting to see how similar Jamini Roy's descriptive reminiscences are to the later Gandhian vision of the ideal village: in a letter to Munnalal Shah dated 4 April 1941, Gandhiji writes: "That village may be regarded as reformed…in which every inhabitant spends some of his time in one or more processes related to cotton, which uses only oil produced in indigenous oil-presses, which consumes only jaggery manufactured in the village itself or in its neighbourhood and only hand-milled flour and hand-pounded rice".

later, especially with the obsessive search for essential form that was closely allied with abbreviation and simplification. The oft-quoted exhortation of his father, 'It is as if we have a book in one hand, and a plough in the other'[6] seems to symbolically point at the very crux of Roy's evolution as an artist: his oeuvre owed almost as much to his study and exposure to the unfolding drama of European Modernism as it did to his intrinsic understanding of the abiding value of folk culture.

This culture, yet unaffected by industrial encroachment, essentially thrived on that basic principle which required a close-knit community to become self-reliant through close dependence on each other. Artisans and craftsmen were innately important to this agrarian economy: carpenters, potters, blacksmiths, wood-carvers, idol-makers, weavers, mat-makers, even *potuas* (*pat*-painters) were not only functionally essential for carrying on daily household activities, but also provided an aesthetic dimension to the day-to-day living. Household decorations like *alpanas* (more often related to religious or social occasions), decorative designs on *sara* and *pirhi*, toys and clay

6 Dey, Bishnu. *Jamini Roy.* p. 18.

figurines, with their motifs/designs—simplified, yet with their referentiality intact—connected the space of both the home and the individual with the throbbing, living culture of the community, to a shared history of familiarity and continuity. The specific case of Beliatore itself was a little unique as well. It was 12 miles away from the nearest railhead, had minimal trade contact with the outside world. It was thus largely free of the economic and social encroachments seen in many other villages of Bengal during the previous century through the growth of markets and the gradual centralisation of trade, which considerably compromised the well-knit village economy, so essential for preservation of the autonomy of village life. The young boy grew up watching firsthand how vessels and other earthenware utensils came out from the potters' wheel, how paddy was husked to make rice, how the Durga idol, in the month of Ashwin, came to life in the hands of the idol-makers from mere heaps of straw and clay. This close familiarity with the processes that yielded the products essential for basic sustenance put his young mind in tune with the unified rhythm of a life in which all occupations were integral and inseparable, where wholeness was brought about by the seamless interdependence of the parts. And this was possibly why the integral harmony and the sense of continuity in folk culture answered to him at a time when he was searching for an avenue away from the conflict and discordance of an urban-industrial culture, away also from the unmoving, non-evolving choices presented by the contemporary art scenario.

And then there were the cradling environs of traditional customs, songs, *palagans* and the narration of *potuas* and other artisans. He would listen to women singing while rhythmically stepping on a *dheki*[7] to thresh and husk paddy, watch them paint *alpanas* on the floor and *basudhara*[8] on the wall (we see the return of related motifs time and again in his paintings), saw yatras and *palagans*,[9] redolent with myths and religion, listened to stories in the same vein from the elderly women in the family. The narration that accompanied the unrolling of

7 Dheki is a manually operated wooden husk-lever used to process rice from paddy, used widely in yesteryears chiefly in the villages of Bengal, Assam and Orissa.

8 Basudhara is an auspicious symbol painted on the wall of a room, usually on occasion of a marriage in the family.

9 Palagan is a narrative folk ballad, immensely popular once in rural Bengal, with subjects drawn from religion, mythology and often popular folk tales. Palagans with devotional content (connected, often, to the lives of Krishna or Chaitanya) were also known as *palakirtan*.

scroll *pats* mostly hinged on these known and well-loved subjects as well, engaging the memory and imagination of generations, and this served in embedding a deep love for myth and tradition in the young boy. We shall see later how the basic tales and motifs of *Krishna-Leela* (narratives relating to the life of Krishna, from his infancy to adulthood, extremely popular then both in *palagans* and as scroll-*pat* subjects) and also tales from the *Ramayana* continued to appear in his later work, when he was already settled in Calcutta for many years. Myths hold together layers of time and generations of people, resist the abruptness of social change, and for Roy they had that added underpinning of nostalgia connected to a vanished, wholesome childhood. In addition to the specifically Hindu myths, traditions and rituals (and some Muslim components), Roy had exposure to the starkly simple lifestyle and culture of the Santhals and other native inhabitants of the area, to their song and dance and other rituals, which were to become lasting reminiscences in his later artworks.

From his very childhood, Jamini Roy was keenly interested in modeling and drawing with whatever available material suited his purpose—in fact he had once made up his mind to be an idol-maker when he would grow up, such was his wonder in watching the Durga image emerge from scratch! He once recounted about how he remained absorbed, for days on end, watching the idol take shape in their *thakurdalan*, often playing truant from school. Even during the puja days, when his friends would frolic along with the beats of the *dhak*, he would pay close attention to how the features of the idol had been fashioned. He would draw dogs, cats and horses on the floor of the *baithak-khana*[10] when he was barely five, and fill in the outlines with red, white and blue pebbles that he had sought out and pocketed from the roadside. When he was older, he sent a painting, called *Samaj* (Society) to a district exhibition of Bankura (notwithstanding his father's unwillingness), and won accolades from the district magistrate, who awarded him with a guinea. This acknowledgement brought about a serious confidence in his own abilities as a painter, and helped him considerably to be able to answer to his calling.

---

10 Baithak-khana was a space where the adult males of the village met for chats and other discussions and played on cards and dice, usually situated at a distance from the main household. Roy's family baithak-khana was three—four minutes walking distance from his home.

Conflict of Creative Identities

Roy came to Calcutta and joined the Government School of Art when he was 16[11]—steeped, still, in the ideal of a no-frills lifestyle—and put up in a single room of North Calcutta with his younger brother Rajani. We must keep in mind that his elder brother was already settled in Calcutta at that time, and was wealthy enough to keep a car. Thus, Roy's choice of a humble rental residence does seem a little surprising, as do his financial struggles to make ends meet during those early days in Calcutta, seemingly without a chaperone. It was a probability that his elder brother had fallen out of favour with his father for violating his wishes and coming over to Calcutta, at the insistence of his maternal uncle, for his school and college education. Jamini Roy himself had referred to this falling-out—'My father could not easily forgive my brother and maternal uncle for this'[12]—as he had no faith in the contemporary system of school education, and did not bother much about Roy's formal schooling as well. But we do get to know that later he did work for

11 The year of his joining would then be 1903, though Partha Mitter maintains that Roy joined the institution in 1906. (See Mitter, Partha, *The Triumph of Modernism*. p. 101.

12 Daw, Prasanta. ed. *Ruptapas Jamini Roy*. p. 297.

his brother's thriving business as a bookseller, delivering books to one Auddy's shop for a sum of about 4 *annas*, before walking all the way to the art school to attend his classes.

Fending for himself in a busy, unfamiliar metropolis could not have been easy for him, but his entry to the Government Art School was a breezy one. Percy Brown, the principal of the school, was amazed by the work of the young boy and allowed him to take lessons at whichever class he chose, waiving off the mandatory admission test.[13] Brown was so impressed with his work that he had also hung a framed painting of Roy's in a classroom when he was still a student. Roy got admitted in the 'Fine Arts' section of the art school, preferring it over the department teaching 'Indian Style of Painting' (a rather artificial and confusing division introduced by the erstwhile principal, E.B. Havell). The Fine Arts section used to run in the Western academic mode, stressing on naturalism and verisimilitude. The curriculum included studies from objects and models—hinging on the eye-fooling, three-dimensional European

13 Since Percy Brown had not yet become the principal in 1903, we can assume that this happened when Roy re-registered himself at a later date.

realistic techniques with stress on perspective and the distribution of light and shade. The reason for Jamini Roy's choice of section could be the fact that students of Fine Arts could find employment relatively easily in various government survey departments. Some of them also received private commissions for painting portraits even during their college days, and the possibility of being able to earn and support himself must have been a decisive factor for the young boy with that independent streak. Towards the end of his art school stint, though, he also took lessons in the Indian Style as well, without completing the full course. We wonder why Roy never received a formal degree from the school even after being associated with it for over a decade, albeit irregularly.

The Government Art School's primary instructional policy was to follow the strict naturalism of the South Kensington School; this was put in place by a previous principal, H. H. Locke, who was preferential to this British academic norm, and was possibly not too sympathetic to the newer art movements that were already inundating the boundaries of tradition not only in Britain, but in the West in general. Jamini Roy gradually became proficient in the illusionist mode and acquired a profound understanding of how ways of seeing, rather than the subject in question, are of prime importance for an artwork. Olito Gilardi, the Italian art teacher under whom Abanindranath Tagore was trained during his early life, used to teach in the school at the time, and in his classes he got the students to paint studies from plaster models. The students sat on very low stools or benches when working, while the considerably tall Gilardi moved about in the classroom, remarking oftentimes that the students were not doing a good job of copying. The young Jamini was quick to point out that the teacher not only had an elevated viewpoint because of his height, but he was also moving about, and thus the stationary students sitting close to the ground could not be expected to see what Gilardi saw and thus their work justifiably differed from what was expected of them. This anecdote clearly refers not only to his early understanding and knowledge of the values of perspective, but also his visual common sense. In fact, Principal Brown was so impressed with his work that he issued a standing instruction to the school's office that he was to be allowed to come and go as he pleased, even if he could not pay his fees. This privilege allowed him to occasionally engage in odd jobs to support himself financially. These jobs were varied and disparate in nature: apart from working for his elder brother, he worked occasionally for a lithographic press at Darjipara in northen Calcutta, having to sit and work on the open porches of houses in a narrow, serpentine lane. He also put colour to the borders of huge *Garanhata* engravings at Bat-tala, working along with maidservants, for a paltry sum. Much later, Bishnu Dey was struck by the similarity of these borders with the border-like thick lines used by Fernand Leger in his paintings: it would be interesting to keep in mind that the French artist was known to be deeply influenced by the Kalighat paintings of Bengal, a style that had had a deep impress on Roy's work as well.

And then there was the Christmas job of painting greeting cards for a Jewish merchant, which yielded 10–12 annas per 100 cards, just enough for a plateful of rice! Certain occupations honed his keen power of observation as well: when he worked at a clothes store in Shyambazar during the evenings, he formed a clear idea about how the taste in clothes, as also the choice of colour, often got influenced by one's profession. Taking a break from the studies of the art school, Roy had even gone to Allahabad to work on lithographs for the Indian Press. At that particular time, they were publishing

Rabindranath's works and Abanindranath's paintings, and it was here in Allahabad that Roy had his first glimpse of Rabindranath. This had a deep effect on him, and he was to become an ardent admirer of Tagore's paintings later in his life.

Roy was also keenly interested in theatre, and it was to remain his only serious involvement apart from painting for about the next two decades. His focus of interest was, however, not the high-brow amateur plays but the professional, popular theatre centered mostly in the stages of the northern part of the city, which could be described as a 'cross between music-hall, pantomime and religious melodrama.'[14] The heightened representation of reality and the vital connect between the actors and audience must have imparted significant lessons to him about the visual correlation of illusion and reality. He regularly painted backdrops for professional theatre, huge 'scenes' which were indispensable props for plays—popular theatre was in its heyday then, attracting large crowds. Roy is known to have painted backdrops and scenes for crowd-pulling productions like Sisir Bhaduri's *Sita* and Jogesh Chowdhury's *Ravan*. He developed a close

14 Dey, Bishnu and John Irwin. *Jamini Roy*. p. 108.

association and certain lasting friendships with theatre personalities and playwrights as well.

Though Jamini Roy had made a name for himself as a painter even during his student days at the Government Art School and was given unique privileges, his relationship with the school remained a fraught one. He himself had confessed that the atmosphere of the school did not answer to his deepest needs, and that he felt like a caged bird, reveling in the illusion of Beliatore—its open skies, forests, the Santhal neighbours, the picture-perfect line of the Bihar hills and the expanse of the green meadows.[15] This clearly reveals the weariness of one who was anyway grappling bravely with a troubled and stressful life in an urban medley, trying to realise his dreams in the city, yet was saddened by the memories of a simpler, wholesome life amid nature that he had to leave behind. And this is probably why he kept on de-registering and re-registering himself in the art school, and thus was associated with the institution for a very long time. Most critics agree that he left the school in 1916, and that too without a formal degree. By then he had already made a name for himself as a portrait painter; Abanindranath Tagore himself called him over

15 Daw, Prasanta, ed. *Ruptapas Jamini* Roy. p. 297.

to their ancestral home at Jorasanko at around 1914 and asked him to paint a likeness of Debendranath Tagore (father of Rabindranath Tagore, philosopher and the co-founder of Brahmo Samaj) from an existing portrait, painted in 1900 by Shashi Hesh.[16] This commission took quite some time, and this might have given him a decisive nudge towards the direction that he was to take in the coming years. During the long period he spent working at Jorasanko, it is extremely probable that he came in contact with the paintings of Sunayani Devi,[17] Abanindranath's sister, who is thought to be the first artist to utilise the idiom of folk art ever. Her paintings were displayed to the guests in Jorasanko by her brothers, Abanindranath and Gaganendranath, and Jamini Roy must have been deeply influenced by her use of the folk form and elements, though his own style was entirely different at that particular point of time.

The technique he was practising then was still close to the naturalist painters. Apart from portraits, he had worked on numerous landscapes in which,

---

16 This huge portrait of Debendranath Tagore is now at *Bangiya Sahitya Parishad*, Kolkata.

17 Sunayani Devi was possibly born in 1881, which would make her six years elder to Jamini Roy. See Som, Sovon. *Shilpi, Shilpo O Somaj*. p. 82.

interestingly, he had already started to veer away from the pressing need of verisimilitude and fine finish—in these we see him experimenting with avant-garde Western artistic techniques, some of them post-Impressionistic exercises almost, creating rich surface patterns with saturated hues of thick paint. One may notice striking resemblances with the technique of the pointillists, especially Paul Signac (ref. pic 02). Roy developed a close association with noted Academic-style painters like Hemen Mazumdar, Atul Bose, B.C. Law and Satish Sinha, and became an active member of the Indian Academy of Art, founded by Mazumdar in 1919. Roy was older to the rest of the members at least by 10 years, and Hemen Mazumdar lovingly called him *Jamini da*—this name stuck for the next 50 years with artists and critics irrespective of age. This group met regularly, in the evenings, and had lively discussions on the current state of Indian art; more often, the conversations veered towards contemporary debates on whether the revivalist tendencies of the Bengal School really constituted that largely undefined quality of Indianness, and conversely, whether the pursuit of Western naturalism compromised the nationalist ideals that had steadily burgeoned especially since the

Swadeshi movement. Though Jamini Roy was already known for his naturalistic oils in the Western academic mode, he did have a soft spot for the Indian-style art that had become so popular then, and this was often teasingly mentioned by his genial artist friends. In 1920, this group decided to publish a journal (initially conceived as a quarterly), also called the *Indian Academy of Art*. The chief intention behind the journal was to counteract the influence of *Rupam*[18] that favoured the Bengal School artists. Some of Roy's paintings published in this journal first showed inklings of that slow change in his artistic temperament that was to result in that steep turn which distanced him both from his proficient practice of realism and his sympathies for the spiritually oriented Indian-style art. In the first issue of the journal (January, 1920), an early specimen of Roy's Santhal-themed paintings appeared as a full-colour plate. It was titled *A Divine Moment*, depicting a Santhal mother teaching her child to pray, and an accompanying description pointed out that 'Mr Roy's new method and idea of painting is praiseworthy...

18 *Rupam* was 'an illustrated quarterly journal of Oriental Art, chiefly Indian', edited by Ordhendra C. Gangoly and published by The Indian Society of Oriental Art.

it is neither "Oriental" nor "Modern"...Mr Roy deals with Oriental subjects with some of the ornaments of the Modern school of painting.'[19] This was indeed a notable syncretism of strands drawn from the camps which stood firmly opposed to each other then: he creates here a misty, atmospheric landscape, redolent of the Orientalists, but departs from their habitual idealisation of the past by mooring his work to his childhood observation of real-life Santhal neighbours. This particular category is historically important because of the cue it provides to the early efforts of the artist to fashion his own singular journey even while drawing from opposing artistic styles: we would soon see him set himself free from the influence of both the Oriental and the Western, both the atmospheric water-colour wash and the realistic oil. At around the same time, he had also painted ordinary village folks often engaged in time-defying religious or cultural practices (representative of these would be paintings like *Namaz* and *A Study* of a *Baul Singer* with his characteristic one-stringed *ektara*, both published in the Indian Academy

19 The word 'modern' here refers to the Western modes of realism in art, and not to the ideas of modernity in culture, history and art history that we instantly and habitually tend to connect it with.

of Art). Some of his characters were dispossessed and marginal as well, though erect with individualism—this indicated, with some clarity, the direction his art was to take in the coming days. His paintings on the Santhals often has a romantic take; depiction of the brave and fearless tribe close to the rhythms of the soil often carries an unvoiced comparison between 'nature' and 'nurture', with the scales heavily tilted towards the former. That is possibly why the erotic underpinning often noticed by critics in this series[20] seems to be a misnomer. What is natural and unremarkable in a state of nature becomes differently connotational within a space of culture (we may recall the erotic obsession of the city-bred for the scantily clad Santhal women depicted in several books and films, especially *Aranyer Din Ratri* by Sunil Gangopadhyay and its film adaptation by Satyajit Ray). The ordinary and the habitual become sexually titillating, depending on the cultural context of the viewer. The romance involved in the image-making does indicate that the artist too was a tad removed from reality, by being able to idealise

20 For example, Partha Mitter describes Roy's representation of Santhal women as being 'redolent of eroticism.' Mitter. *The Triumph of Modernism*. p. 103.

it thus. It is a space of nostalgia that separated him from that state of oneness with unspoilt nature that he wished to recapture through these simple and free people whom he knew so well once.

In 1921, when the Indian Academy of Art was about to stop further publication due to dire shortage of funds, some of the members formed the Society of Fine Arts, chiefly to ensure the arrangement of an annual all-India art exhibition every year, and Jamini Roy became its honorary secretary. Percy Brown, the principal of Government Art School, allowed the group to use the premises of the school for what was to be the first all-India exhibition in Calcutta, welcoming artworks from both the mutually opposed camps. Roy was indeed a singular figure in those contested times of raging aesthetic debates who had been close to both sides (it is a well-known fact that he was a favourite of Abanindranath Tagore) and combined elements of both in his own early works.

This was also a period of great turmoil for Roy, for it opened up several directional pulls: the time had come to locate his choice. It could not have been easy for him as he had married Anandamoyee Devi while he was still a student, and had to support a family mainly from his income from portrait commissions. He had painted numerous portraits in his lifetime—a few of these were executed even after he had shifted to his folk-themed paintings. Roy painted portraits of Jadunath Sarkar, Sarat Chandra Chattopadhyay, Rabindranath Tagore and M.K. Gandhi, among many other prominent personages, and the famous art critic O.C. Gangoly was so taken by his skills that he got the portrait of his parents painted by him. But at that particular point of time, he was growing increasingly restless with the prevailing art scenario, and understood that he could identify with none of the current trends. He was anyway wary about the historicism of the Orientalists, in spite of agreeing in spirit with the need to search for an authentic medium. For him, the frescoes of Ajanta, the Mughal and Rajput miniatures (from which the Orientalists drew their main inspiration) were as alien to contemporary Bengal as Western academism was, since none of these were embedded in the climate, culture and society of Bengal, and thus could not be a natural inheritance with live roots to the soil. Though not a 'sudden repudiation', he had been deeply concerned with the inadequacy of all the available choices for quite some time then—this period brought about that decisive moment of transformation when he abandoned the much-trodden ways and turned to look closely at the living folk traditions of Bengal. These were the arts and crafts which unified the community through visual and linguistic signifiers of a shared culture, embedded over generations. In the mid-1920s, Roy roamed around the villages of Bengal to collect *pats* from the practicing *patuas*, not only to build up an invaluable collection (which later adorned an entire room in his studio), but also to reconnect with their distinctive creative modes. Apart from the *pats* and toys and figurines, he also had an impressive collection of Chitpur woodcuts and coloured lithographs, indicating his interest in the movement and value of lines. In fact, as Mulk Raj Anand had noted, he had, in his work, consciously revived that respect for the quality of line 'which is an Indian speciality, the result perhaps of centuries of effort to attain rhythm, almost as though it were a spiritual exercise.'[21]

What he was seeking for were, among other things, ways to contest the mediation of temporality and change by connecting to the vital rhythms that throbbed through the simple, basic pattern of life. He wanted to restore that pre-colonial sense of a united community

21 Anand, Mulk Raj. *Jamini Roy*. p. 48.

in his art, one that had been disrupted by the British rule, effecting the alienation of the urban from their deeper cultural roots. Urbanity had become the very face of change, existing almost as a counterpoint to this placid continuity. Thus Bengal villages, with their nurturing of folk traditions, became a natural choice of reference. But it is also important to remember that for all his rural roots, his years in Calcutta (especially his residence in Ananda Chatterjee Lane in Bagbazar, with its proximity to most of the cultural hubs, including the commercial theatres) and his association with the intellectual glitterati from home and abroad had turned him into the proverbial urban gentleman in his later years who could seamlessly adapt to the very different culture of the city. As his fame gradually mounted, his humble home in that narrow Bagbazar lane with 'its two green street doors, its barred windows, its narrow white-washed roofs, squeezed among crowded neighbours'[22] gradually became a haven for intellectuals and art lovers.

Such associations did not, however, mediate with his essential simplicity of dress and manners. He continued to wear short garments made of coarse material over borderless *dhoti*s (these were always invariably white)

22 Milford, Mary. *A Modern Primitive*. p. 338.

with *taltala* slippers, maybe with the addition of a plain grey *alowan* in winter, even when he had attained the height of fame and recognition. This can be seen in connection with that interesting juxtaposition of identities which we notice time and again in Roy's career. We must keep in mind that the folk art forms intrinsically harbour not only simplicity, but also *simplification* and abbreviation of forms—the latter being the mainstay of most modernist art movements in the West. Jamini Roy, with his close familiarity with the contemporary Western art waves, had located this feature in folk art, had shared the urban artists' weariness with a mechanised civilisation and their quest for wholeness and simplicity in earlier art forms: only in his case this was an evolved revisit to the experiences of an earlier self. He had already been familiar with the *pats* of rural Bengal since his childhood, but his early years in Calcutta introduced him to a unique variety where the folk and the urban intersected: the Kalighat *pats*. These were produced by *patua*s from different villages of Bengal who settled near the temple of Kalighat and catered to the teeming demand of the pilgrims who would carry home these cheaply priced paintings as souvenirs. The traditional, rural art of the *pat* was extensively recalibrated by the urban space and the economics of a thriving market. The folk elements inherent in their simplified forms, fast brushing and vibrant palette, often combined with urban social narratives, especially in the later days. Though Roy did not consider these to belong to the same category of authentic folk *pats*, the deep influence of Kalighat *pats* in his work cannot be overemphasised. In the mid-1920s, there ensued a short-lived phase when his works turned austere and almost monochromatic. During this phase we notice the clear influence of the Kalighat *pats* in his representations of mother and child, seated women and *bauls*, where he attempts to capture the figural volume with fast-moving lines as the Kalighat painters did.

As Suhrawardy had emphasised once, it was from the remarkably expressionist *pats* of the Bengal villages that Roy had learnt the secret of the fundamental rapid line and the expressive contour that enclosed the human form in one vital sweep.[23] Later in the 1920s, the early paintings on the Santhals, along with other works, were exhibited at a show in 1929, organised by Alfred Henry Watson who was then the English editor of the *Statesman* newspaper. Mukul Dey, the principal of the Government Art School then, admired Roy in spite

23 Suhrawardy, Shahid. *The Art of Jamini Roy*. p. 125.

of being an Orientalist himself and was instrumental in arranging this show at the school premises. At the end of the show, Dey came and showered the artist—who was sitting on the floor, engrossed with paper and paint—with banknotes received as proceeds from the sale of his paintings.[24] But it was his next exhibition the year after, at the Indian Society of Oriental Art, which communicated the unique vigour of his recently arrived-at visual idiom. Interestingly, this exhibition also included three panels worked on by folk painters; though it is said that he had retained control over these by putting finishing touches to the panels himself. This co-siting of his own works with those of the traditional folk painters also indicates an identification which was not only an instinctive, internal feeling, but one which could now be publicly proclaimed. We must keep in mind that Jamini Roy had called himself a *patua* on more than one occasion. This self-identification was not limited simply to similar themes, techniques or concerns, but included identical manners of 'production' as well. He used to refer to the prolificacy and repetitiveness of the art practice of traditional *patuas* in order to justify both his own habit of using

24 Mitter, Partha. *The Triumph of Modernism*, p. 110.

similar images repeatedly, and the enormous number of paintings he produced.

This change of direction did incite an attitude of ambivalence in some of his patrons, though it suddenly seemed that he 'could do no better than the crude and barbarous village folk whose wares you could buy for pennies at every country fair.'[25] It is clear thus that his choice involved much more than a change of idiom. It was connected with deeper questions of value and significance of art, and the factors that constituted them, questions that would be addressed in due time by the very nature of his art practice.

The sharp change in artistic direction was also accompanied by a transformation in his palette. Though initially he went through a phase of austere, almost monochromatic experiments, most of which consisted of grey wash and black lines (*Nayika from Kalighat*, ref. pic 11 for example), he shifted later to a limited range of colours. He restricted himself only to seven basic colours—Indian red, cadmium green, yellow ochre, charcoal grey, vermilion, cobalt blue and white. Black was used for drawing the outlines. The nature of pigments too altered significantly. He completely

25 Leyden, R.V. *Jamini Roy*. p. 37.

departed from the readymade, commercially produced paints, mostly European and Chinese, which were both easy to use and to procure, and turned to indigenous pigments that the traditional *patuas* used for their art. These had to be painstakingly made from naturally occurring sources, usually by the artist himself. *Holi mati* was used to make yellow ochre and *gerimati* for Indian red, a mercury composition known as *hingul* provided the basic ingredient for vermilion. Blue was obtained from indigo and greenish stones, grey from alluvial mud, white from white clay/common chalk, while black was sourced from burnt coconut shells and lamp black from the soot at the back of cooking vessels. But he did differ from the traditional *patuas* in the use of brush—for a certain time, he still employed the European brush and not the traditional goat-hair brush that the *patuas* used. They also favoured the gum used from unripe *bel* (wood-apple) fruits, while Roy used to make glue by boiling tamarind seeds in water,[26] though he shifted to sirish-glue later as the earlier concoction turned the colours darker after a certain time. His

26 This was also another well-known process of glue preparation in Bengal. After boiling the tamarind seeds in water the glutinous pulp obtained was kept for a week in water before use.

supports were provided usually by the cheap, homespun cloth of his village which he would then prepare with a layer of alluvial soil and cow dung, and then whitewash the surface. He is also known to have used cheap three-ply wood, handmade cardboard, or the rough side of poster paper. Thus, this choice of treading an entirely variant artistic path was fraught with difficulties that not only jeopardised his living, but also demanded much more industrious involvement than a simple shift to a changed set of visual idioms.

Roy had become progressively wary about the practice of reproducing the illusion of a three-dimensional visual experience on a flat pictorial surface. In his works he broke away completely from this illusory apparatus and used flat colours enclosed in dark contour lines within a predominantly two-dimensional frame with no intention to capture the illusion-inducing apparatus of realism like volume or perspective. Details were reduced to the bare minimum, thus aiming to capture what Clive Bell would have called 'significant form'. But in quite a number of paintings he does break away from this juxtaposition of even colours by using stippling or daubs in the background, thus creating a pictorial surface with a sense of unevenness. His subjects were mostly drawn from the communitarian interpretation of religious mythology: the gods are almost human in his works, as is common in the village tales. He painted the drama around Krishna's life—a subject that never wanes from its popularity, especially in Bengal—and we see him with Yashoda, with Gopinis and also as the saviour. Episodes from the *Ramayana* that he frequently painted (K. C. Das, the famous confectioner of Calcutta, commissioned an entire series of panels on the *Ramayana*) have the same stress on the humanness of the conceptually divine figures. He often painted the pivotal dramatic moments of the epic like Ravana's abduction of Sita (ref. pic 20), or Sita's *Agnipareeksha* (ref. pic 23), and often chose themes that depicted collective cultural/religious activities like kirtan processions and Santhal dance.

By the 1930s the circle of Roy's close acquaintances grew considerably, as did the appreciation for his paintings. The older artist friends did still continue to meet on full moon nights—the group was then called *Shilpi Chakra*—and elaborate discussions on art were accompanied by sumptuous food. But by then he had also developed close friendships with avant-garde poets, critics and noted aesthetes like Bishnu Dey, Sudhindranath Dutta, Shahid Suhrawardy and Stella Kramrisch among others, and these associations helped the artist in several ways. In fact, it was Kramrisch who encouraged him to arrange a show of his works at his own residence at Ananda Chatterjee Lane in 1931 (which became a regular, biannual event for some years). This was a unique show in the sense that the venue was unlike a conventional exhibition hall, and the mounting of the show, including the careful creation of atmosphere, was totally unlike any that Calcutta had experienced before. The exhibited paintings had *pradeeps* (small earthenware oil-and-wick lamps) with their muted glow below each, *dhuno* (Indian frankincense) was burning in incense burners, the viewers were to sit not in chairs, but on square rectangular mats (*asans*) in the manner typical to rural Bengali households. An extensive alpana was created on the courtyard which one had to cross in order to reach the exhibition area. Shanta Devi, who reviewed the exhibition in an issue of *Prabasi* (a popular Bengali magazine with considerable outreach in its own time), noted how the carefully created atmosphere of rural domesticity perfectly complemented the folk-themed paintings that were put up as exhibits in the uniquely themed show. Looking back today, it does appear to us to be an ingeniously conceived installation with interactive spaces for the viewers, the creation of an area of immersive experience that worked only on the basis of the site-specific cues provided. There was a separate room in which Roy's collection of traditional Bengal *pats* were on display as well. This close approximation to a slice of rural Bengal within a busy North Calcutta lane was an interesting interface of the imaginary and the real, the awareness of each state mediating with the other and bringing into the equation the inevitable strands of nostalgia and longing for the non-present. In fact, different kinds of co-presences have characterised Jamini Roy's works almost always: the present attends the past, the urban negotiates with the rural.

Rabindranath Tagore had come to visit Roy and see his paintings at his home: it is said that he sat waiting on a chowki for Jamini Roy, who was then out shopping for the marriage of his eldest daughter. On his return, he saw a sizeable crowd in his lane who had gathered to see the poet but Roy had no idea that it was his house that the poet was in! It is also said that Tagore wanted him to join Santiniketan, but Roy refused, perhaps anticipating a stunt of artistic growth that might come about under the shadow of a creative giant. In fact, Roy is known to have asked Tagore to 'abandon Santiniketan, stop being 'Gurudeva' and devote himself solely to painting.'[27] Roy was fascinated by Tagore's paintings, especially what he called the 'lively, spirited backbone' that differentiated his work from all else. Tagore's letters (written during the final months of his life) to Roy indicate that the poet, too, greatly valued this appreciation: in one of these letters (dated 25 May 1941), he says, 'this evidence, from someone as talented as you, is a matter of great assurance to me.'

The 1937 show of Roy's works at the gallery of Indian Society of Oriental Art at Samabay Mansion unequivocally established his growing fame. This exhibition remained memorable for him chiefly for the hearty appreciation he received from Gaganendranath Tagore, who had also purchased Roy's *Mother and Child*. Gaganendranath was considerably ill at the time of this exhibition and had lost his power of speech due to paralysis. He came to see the exhibition nevertheless, and was so overwhelmed with the works that he embraced the artist with his face awash with flowing

27 Datta, Meenakshi. The Popular Art of Jamini Roy: Reminiscences. p. 281.

tears. Roy was to recount this experience many a time later in his life (it acquired a deeper and more poignant dimension especially because Gaganendranath passed away the year after) and remembered the veteran artist's reaction as a kind of blessing: 'He praised my work with his tears, communicated to me the words of his heart—how much love and affection he had for me.'[28]

Soon afterwards, in 1938, he had another notable exhibition at sculptor Kshitish Chandra Roy's studio at British Indian Street. These two significant back-to-back shows did considerably extend his reputation; they also consolidated his connections with the noted intellectuals of Calcutta, many of whom were from the West and adored his work. Prominent among them were Lindsay Emerson, the British assistant editor of *The Statesman*, his Bengali wife Mrinalini Emerson, Maie Casey (wife of the last Lieutenant Governor of Bengal) John Irwin and Mary Milford. Milford, in a reminiscence on the artist that she published in 1944 in London, recalled[29] how the artist would paint all day, propped by a bolster, surrounded by earthen pots of bright colours. In his house, as she remembered, his

28 Daw, Prasanta. *Ruptapas Jamini Roy*. p. 271.

29 Milford, Mary. *A Modern Primitive*. p. 340.

works were hung in three rooms, each room devoted to a different style: the first room had his earlier Kalighat-inspired works, the second displayed his experiments with the French impressionistic mode (ref. pic 15), and also some pointillist landscapes in bright primary colours (it is interesting to note that the early portraits, which he had become renowned for, went unrepresented in this display). The third room was for his major works in the folk idiom, steeped in mythology. Roy was also visited at his home by illustrious guests such as the British biologist J.B.S Haldane, novelist E.M. Forster and the Soviet film director Vsevolod Pudovkin. An interesting anecdote describes how both Pudovkin and actor Nikolai Cherkasov (the two were co-actors in Eisenstein's *Ivan the Terrible*) wanted to buy the same Roy painting, of a blue-veiled woman. Cherkasov had to be content with another almost similar painting, as Pudovkin had chosen first. Both were happy: they felt as if the two painted women were sisters, one would go to Moscow with the director, and the other would accompany the actor to Leningrad![30]

We do not know whether it was the cultural difference that provided an extra dimension of fascination to his

30 Dey, Bishnu. *Jamini Roy*. pp. 47–48.

overseas admirers, or whether Roy's works provided to them a welcome change from the pan-Indian phenomenon of painting in the fashion of Western modernists. Rolf Italiaander, the German writer and director (who called Roy the 'Great Master') was pained to see in the 32nd Exhibition of All India Fine Arts and Crafts Society (AIFACS) 'only ten percent of Indian motifs',[31] amid artworks mostly following European stylistics, both old and new. It is understandable, thus, how the indigenous vein of Roy's paintings would be especially impressive to those who were already overtly familiar with what was happening in the West–Indian paintings following the Western idiom hardly had any fresh appeal for them. During the Second World War, the much-debated book of novelist Beverley Nichols, *Verdict on India*, proclaimed that there was 'only one artist of any consequence, by name Jamini Roy' while 'India was an artistic desert…the artist was on the level with the untouchable.'[32] While almost comically displaying his ignorance about the Indian condition (and compounding it further by insinuating Jinnah's greatness and Gandhi's ineffectuality), these lines did go

31 Italiaander, Rolf. *Meeting with a Great Master*. p. 42.

32 Nichols, Beverley. *Verdict on India*. p. 116.

a long way to spread Roy's fame internationally. Bishnu De had pointed out that lakhs of copies of the book were sold—these must have considerably influenced overseas opinion about the artist. *Horizon*, the influential literary magazine of London, carried Mary Milford's essay on Roy titled 'The Modern Primitive', thus introducing him to the British intellectuals. The war brought numerous British and American army personnel to Calcutta, many of whom purchased Roy's paintings and sent them home. In fact, Roy seems to have kept an open house then, visited by a steady stream of both Indians and foreigners, many of whom bought his artworks that remained remarkably low-priced.

In 1942, Calcutta was overwhelmed with the scare of bombing by Japanese fighter jets. Like many others, Jamini Roy, too, left the city under pressure from his relatives, though he was not too keen to leave behind his huge group of friends and the regular, fruitful interactions he had with them. He went back to his village, Beliatore, for a few months: this was the last time he would see his native place, for he never went back to Beliatore again in his lifetime. But this period was, surprisingly, not at all productive for him, though he was reunited with his beloved birthplace which had been inspirational for him throughout. As his letters to various people written during this period suggest, he was unable to continue to paint to his satisfaction at least in the initial days, though he did finish a number of sculptures as well as paintings later during this period. In a letter to Bishnu Dey (dated 9 September 1942) he clearly states that he misses his earlier practice of target-oriented work. 'I work for my livelihood. That is what is missing now. Working simply for the sake of work, art for art's sake, is that higher state I have not been able to reach yet…the arrangement of the room where the painting is placed matters a lot… without such an environment I cannot find the strength to work, it becomes directionless.' It does seem that he was missing not only his familiar workstation at his Calcutta home, but also the regular demand for his paintings, to cater to which he had to work tireless hours earlier. The war situation, coupled with his displacement from the city, considerably lessened this 'need' to work, and his letters also indicate a shortage of money which his friends in the city tried to mitigate by helping to sell his paintings which he would send over by post. Roy gratefully acknowledges the significant role of his friends in the same letter: 'My friends signify the real food, clothes, and wealth in my life.' After his return to Calcutta, he could, however, tune back with ease to his busy, productive life, settling again to work in his beloved studio in the dark, narrow serpentine lane of North Calcutta, where the sunlight hardly ever entered.

Another major solo show of Roy's paintings was held at the Society of Oriental Art in 1944, which was supposed to be accompanied by an elaborate catalogue with plates of his paintings. But the idea of the illustrated portfolio had to be dropped as Roy felt deeply uncomfortable with the printing of the images, and was possibly anxious about the accuracy of colour in the reproductions. He even sent back the agreement form of the Society as he was eerily convinced that 'the publication of this monograph could actually become the reason of my death—this matter disturbs my mind so much that my frail health is ill-equipped to tolerate it.'[33] This reaction, which does seem disproportionately severe, may have been linked to an edginess induced in him by contemporary adverse opinions about his work. It would not be easy for us to understand how an ageing, renowned artist, wary of criticism, would cautiously steer clear of controversies generated by possible imperfections in the printed images, at a time

33 Letter to Bishnu De, dated 5 December 1944.

when his line of work was already being criticised at various quarters. Roy seems to be especially concerned about the attitude of the Santiniketan painters towards his art, a specimen of which clearly sums up the berating stand that must have been around for some time: Benodebehari Mukherjee, in one of his articles,[34] unequivocally states that 'In his artistic career there is no evolution, only change. His oil paintings are imitations of Abanindranath,[35] and also show his following of Western Impressionism—at every step he is looking for something new…such rapid change has been able to evoke curiosity in us; but we do not get to see the artist's own vision. From the point of view of *rasa*, there is nothing new in his works.' Even Nandalal Bose had commented, in reference to Gurusaday Dutt (whose collection of folk art and crafts were exhibited in the Society of Oriental Art right after Roy's show in 1931) that Dutt was giving the *pats* more importance than they deserved—he clearly did not accept Dutt's thesis that the *pats* represented the 'art language' of the country.

34 Published in *Anandabazar Patrika*, 18 February 1945.

35 It is indeed perplexing to think why Mukherjee would draw a parallel here with Abanindranath, whose shunning of oil paint was well known, and had become one of the main features of the Bengal School.

His following comments clearly allude to Roy, without naming him:

'Though certain artists have been able to express their feelings through the *pats*, one cannot be too enthusiastic about such originality. It is only arbitrary work, without scientific basis. Therefore it cannot last. The *pat* gives a flat treatment. We are familiar with several such modes of flat treatment. But the *patuas* who do not have any scientific basis cannot be a source of inspiration for any other artists.'[36]

We can perhaps understand now why Suhrawardy, in his *Prefaces*, said that for years, Roy was held to be a fanatic who was pursuing originality in vain.

But Roy's uneasiness with permitting printed reproductions of his works could also be related to his own practice of repeating and reproducing the same images or image configurations, producing numerous 'copies' as it were, to cater to the ever-increasing demand, leading to the legend that he had set up a factory at his house! It is possible that he did not want his paintings to be freely available to the public through the colour plates which were to be printed in the proposed book,

36 Dutt, Gurusaday. *Folk Arts and Crafts of Bengal: The Collected Papers*. pp. xvii–xix.

especially because his works were still low-priced and were affordable even to the middle class. But he was also deeply saddened by the rift this incident caused between him and his well-wishers, particularly Stella Kramrisch, who were irked with his wavering during the initial phases of the proposed project before the decisive denial came. It is known that he had become reticent in his later years and seldom went out of his house. He was not too fond of travelling—in fact he had never traveled out of India[37]—and got increasingly self-absorbed within the charmed, reassuring circle of his work in his beloved studio. Austin Coates once described an amazing experience he had had with Jamini Roy[38]: he once arrived at Roy's studio to see him holding a first-class return sleeper ticket to Delhi in his hand; he was supposed to go and receive the decoration that the Nehru government had conferred on him. But he refused to make the journey, saying that 'If they want to give it to me, let them send it'. The matter had to be settled finally in accordance to his wishes.

37 In spite of never having travelled abroad, Jamini Roy had a few significant exhibitions overseas: in 1946 his works were shown at the Arcade Gallery in London (which was inaugurated by the novelist E.M. Forster), and later, in New York, in 1953 and 1957.

38 Coates, Austin. *The Peasant Painter*. p. 51.

In 1949 Jamini Roy relocated to his own two-storied house designed by himself at Dihi Sreerampore Road, Ballygunge, where the entire ground floor was devoted to his paintings. There were rooms for the display of his works, with simple whitewashed walls and low wooden seating. It was something akin to a permanent exhibition, benefitting viewers and buyers alike, reducing somewhat the need for frequent public shows. Some of his friends, like Buddhadev Bose, believing that Roy's spirit and lifestyle belonged firmly to the north Calcutta neighbourhood, even felt dejected at his relocation. Material plenitude was not something that found a natural place in his lifestyle (though he was far from averse to rightful earning)—his interiors were austere, tidy, the piles of paintings were perfectly arranged and the house always remained meticulously clean. This sense of sufficiency in what is simple and possibly unfashionable, coupled with his traditional, often conservative take on life, was what probably struck his friends as a temperament that would not comfortably inhabit his large house, situated in a wide-open area of fashionable Ballygunge. In fact, when the street of his new house was renamed later to Ballygunge Place East in 1956, he seemed to ignore this rechristening entirely;

till the very end of his life almost all his correspondences bore the earlier address of Dihi Sreerampore Lane. This preference could be traced to a subconscious appreciation of how the previous name held the remembrance of the forgotten, pre-urbanised origin of the region—*Dihi* literally means a group of villages, and it is possible that he liked to remind himself, and others, of the rural roots of the now fashionable region that he lived in by continuing to use the earlier name with its resonance of yesteryears.

The fact that he created several paintings out of the same image-configurations has been commented on by many critics, often with a harsh edge. It is possible that the huge demand for his paintings had necessitated this, as it did the collaborative system of working that he followed in his later days. Roy's eldest son, Jimoot, who had been an able assistant to his father, had died mysteriously in the woods near Beliatore when he was only sixteen. Later, however, his youngest son Patal (Amiya Roy) became proficient enough to assist his father. It is said that he had taught Patal the structure and basic forms that he used. Patal would fill the colours in many of the works to which Roy would then put the finishing touches, and sign. Roy did not ever think that there was anything wrong in such a system: he even referred to the painters' guilds of medieval Europe, citing that students often did the major work on a painting under the guidance of a master painter, who would then finish the painting and sign it. In fact, the making of Mughal painting largely shared the same collective character as well. Akbar had a royal artistic studio—the *tasbirkhana*—where more than a hundred craftsmen and artists of varying skill were employed to illustrate manuscripts, paint portraits and other artworks.

Jamini Roy had made it adequately clear that it was precisely this collective system that made possible the production of the staggering volume of paintings which, in its turn, allowed him to keep the prices of his paintings affordable. Affordability seems to be the key factor here: he had unequivocally declared once, 'What I want is, instead of hanging calendars in the walls of homes, let them hang a *pat* painted by me. That is precisely why I sell these at low prices. Unless the number increases, how could I keep up the supply?'[39] Even if we are to consider his justification of this collective system of production as an ingenious marketing strategy (as has been done by quite a few) it can hardly be debated that

39 Sanyal, Bhabesh. *Kichhu Smriti*. p. 77.

he had indeed been concerned with the question of the integral connection of art with lived life. Roy had seen first-hand how folk art permeated rural life in a quiet, imperceptible manner, and possibly wanted to replicate that experience within an urban framework, for his urban clientele who were far removed from the wholesome rural interface of art and life. One would also wonder whether he was intentionally undermining that unique singularity of an artwork which became a marker of its value, that *aura*[40] of a painting which would be compromised by reproductions. Was he interrogating, then, the value of the signed 'original', as against the work of numerous nameless *patuas*, whose works adorned countless rural homes and gave pleasure to many, in spite of being largely replicatory? This seems to be a complicated interface between an urban-capitalist mediation which located the intrinsic value of art in its unique singularity that can be *possessed*, and those unnamed, much-replicated traditions of folk art that sought to find the pleasure of art in familiar forms and unifying themes. These were unaffected by this very different pleasure of possessing the original,

40 See Benjamin, Walter. '*The Work of Art in the Age of Mechanical Reproduction*', in Illuminations. p. 221.

as there would be no original. Roy was perhaps drawn towards this anonymity of the folk artists, and the value created only through the use of line, form, colour and narrative, and not through any extra-textual 'signature', that appealed to the life of the community. The fact that his own paintings sold largely because of the name he had made for himself remains as a counter-narrative though: he was hardly an anonymous *patua*, and he wanted to be, and was, celebrated for his originality. But such are the downsides of the cultural displacement that he possibly tried to resist in his art. The value associated with originality and individuality is typically related to a capitalist urban–industrial culture, and in spite of his deep connections to Bengal's rural–agrarian rhythms, he had settled in and responded readily to the conditions of a city life. And that is possibly why the folk/urban interface never reaches a point of contestation in his life. The imagined binaries flow into each other, coalesce and frame each other: just as folk art, folk motifs surrounded him, not only in his artworks and aesthetic discussions, but physically, in his city studio. In the same manner, his urban refinement sets apart his artworks from the folk, rehabilitates them almost, from the habitual anonymity of the *patuas*. It is also a point of contention whether after a certain period, when his art was settled in his mature, signature style, he was in fact dictated by the demands of the market which deterred him from further experimentation, and stranded his art in a doldrum of schematic stillness.

Jamini Roy was conferred the Padma Bhushan by the Government of India in 1955, was elected the Fellow of Lalit Kala Akademi the following year and was honoured by the Akademi in a ceremony right at his residence in 1961. This was also the time when he was experimenting with mosaic-like effects in his works. In this, he was adequately assisted by his son Amiya, who had achieved proficiency in working with mosaic tiles himself. The square subdivisions (inspired by the tesserae[41] of Byzantine mosaics) employed in these paintings imparted texture to his works, as well as a further geometric dimension in tune with the formal austerity. The same intent possibly worked when he chose bamboo or palm-leaf matting to paint on—it had a similar texture of small squares, and Roy was possibly experimenting with this geometrical symmetry and its interface with the schematic nature of his paintings

41 Tesserae are small pieces of glass, stone, ceramic, or other material used in Byzantine mosaics, usually in the shape of a cube.

which anyway was based closely on a geometry of its own. The subjects he chose were interesting as well: he painted the usual religious icons of Byzantine mosaics such as Christ on the Cross—he also has works of Christ carrying a transparent cross—but alongside, he worked with such themes too as were rooted in Bengal myths and folklore such as *Ganesh-Janani* (ref. pic 14) and *Mahadev o Ganesh*. It did seem, in case of *Ganesh-Janani*, as if he was trying to 'translate the Byzantine Madonna into indigenous terms'.[42] In fact, Jamini Roy had extensively worked with the figure of Christ and the Christ-myths since the 1940s. This seems surprising because he had never even read the New Testament. There is a critical view which suggests that he had adopted the Christ theme so that his paintings would have an additional appeal to the Christian British and American soldiers who thronged Calcutta during the Second World War, and thus would find a ready market among them. It is possible that the financial success of this series may have prompted him to continue with the Christ theme in a large number of paintings. But Roy's reason was that he wanted to apply his new technique to the treatment of a subject naturally remote from the culture and history

42 Som, Sovon. *Jamini Royer Chhabi: Riti o Tatporjo*. p. 111.

he was rooted to, and find out whether it worked as well as it did on subjects closer to his direct lived experience. The post-Renaissance illusionist paintings of Western Europe had appeared to him to be products influenced by the ethos of an industrial–capitalist society, severed from spiritual roots. That is possibly why Roy was attracted to the pre-Renaissance European art, especially to the Byzantine icons. Bishnu Dey tells us about his child-like delight at finding the corroboration of his own thoughts in a book on Byzantine art.

But 1960s onwards, his health was in a state of gradual decline: it is possible that his health suffered because of the enormous pressure he put on himself to continue to keep on painting to cater to the increasing demand. Keeping in mind his long urban settlement and close connection with intellectuals and modernists of both India and abroad, it would indeed be perplexing to note that he had no faith in the advances of modern medicine. He had refused to take any vaccines in his entire life, and relied mainly on homoeopathy. It was necessary for him to undergo a surgery, though, when he was in his seventies, which further broke down his constitution. The unremitted hours that he devoted to his work had to be curtailed:

earlier, he used to come down to his studio right after breakfast and continued work throughout the day, with a short nap on the couch after a simple lunch. Ill health necessitated him to take rest frequently, yet he could not but continue with his work. The artist's grandson Debabrata Roy, in an interview, reminisced about Roy's incredible commitment to his work. He also recounted about how the artist would be displeased even with the slightest disorganisation in the household, such was his insistence on order and discipline.

Buddhadev Bose describes him three years before his death as a wizened man with dull eyes and wrinkled skin, on the verge of dementia, who, nevertheless, still continued to paint, then on a piece of palm-leaf matting.[43] *The Last Supper* was possibly the last work of the painter (though he worked on several versions of the same theme earlier,[44] some of these on palm-leaf matting as well) which was left unfinished—the 7/2.4 ft work had been started by the artist only about a week before his death. The other similarly themed works typically depict

43 Bose, Buddhadev. *Dhanya Jamini Roy*. p. 122.

44 One version of Roy's Last Supper paintings is at St. Paul's Cathedral, Kolkata, in which only Christ's face is painted frontally while the disciples' faces are turned towards him, thus visible to the viewers in profile.

Christ and his 12 disciples rowed up in a straight line, with identical faces and the same wide eyes with almost geometric symmetry. It is, as if, the schematic repetition of figures has the effect of an incantation, which further served to reinforce the iconic effect of the paintings.

Jamini Roy died on 24 April 1972, after having suffered for over a year from bronchial pneumonia and other age-related ailments. In December 1976, Roy's artworks were declared as a 'national treasure' by the Government of India.[45] It is somewhat surprising that Roy's work did not culminate in a direct legacy to the later generations of Indian artists, though the spirit had continued to inspire many. This may have been due to what Suhrawardy called Roy's 'unshared communion' with the object of his quest,[46] a connection with his art that continued to remain deeply personal to the self-effacing and ineloquent artist. Much has been written about his art, in fact he is one of the most discussed artists of his times, but it is through the memoirs and reminiscences of close friends, acquaintances and fellow

45 The other artists whose works are also considered as 'national treasure' are Raja Ravi Varma, Rabindranath Tagore, Amrita Shergil, Abanindranath Tagore, Gaganendranath Tagore, Nandalal Bose, Nicholas Roerich and Sailoz Mookherjea.

46 Suhrawardy, Shahid. *'The Art of Jamini Roy' in Prefaces*. p. 116.

artists that we are allowed glimpses at what the artistic process really meant to the self-effacing artist who was so drawn to seclusion. Notwithstanding the collective, collaborative nature that became a hallmark of his art practice, and also his oft-repeated exhortations that painting was a 'profession' to him, the actual, absorbed moments of connecting to the first conceptions were almost meditative. Most artists experience such moments of communion when emotions become images, but in case of Jamini Roy, interiorised as he was, these must have been intense and pervasive. We are told[47] that he would rise long before first light and sit on the floor of the studio in total darkness, thinking. As the first light of dawn came in through the small vent in the roof, the pictures in his studio would dimly appear—only the lines first, without any colour—then as the day brightened, the colours would emerge gradually. The artist would begin his day, in perfect tune with the rhythms of nature, colour and line.

And this is how we would like to remember him.

47 Coates, Austin. *The Peasant Painter*. p. 51.

TRANSLATING THE FOLK

When an artist, well settled in a particular genre and earning comfortably out of it, decides to travel along an entirely variant direction and succeeds in creating a highly individual artistic idiom, such a departure becomes a moment of history. And like all historical moments, it has its antecedents and preconditions, much of which is subsumed within the discourse of the artist's conscious choice. But consciousness is many-layered, vulnerable to different modes of suggestivities, and configured in complex manners by the negotiations of both the individual and the community: it is thus essential that we try to understand the factors, both individual and social, that led up to Jamini Roy's decisive turn towards the rural and the folk.

We have already observed how this turn was hardly a 'sudden repudiation' as suggested by Archer, but was preceded by a gradual process of disillusionment with the way academic realism was poised to capture the external resemblance of its subject. Reality hardly resides only in the externals, nor does the shape of feelings obediently fall in line with the accurate representation of what is merely seen by the eyes, and this had been an issue most modernist painters had negotiated with in their search for distinct visual languages. In a sense, Jamini Roy's quest was similar to that of Abanindranath and the Orientalists in the way both turned away from naturalism and focused on Indian roots. We must recognise that both the Bengal school artists and Jamini Roy had been a part of the contemporary nationalist imperative in 'dislodging modern art from its western context, in the continuous assertion of cultural difference, and in the ceaseless search for Indian authenticity.'[1] While one concentrated on the revival of ancient myths, narratives and models of earlier art (like the Ajanta murals) which had almost no connection with the culture of Bengal, Roy turned towards the living folk traditions in the villages of Bengal that he had known intimately in his childhood. Whereas Abanindranath and his followers of

1 Guha-Thakurta, Tapati. *Lineages of the Modern in Indian Art: The Making of a National History*. p. 106.

the Bengal school were 'reviving' long-dead traditions buried in the past, Roy was connecting to the folk idiom which was not only kept alive by transmission across generations, but had still been an intrinsic part of life as it was lived in the village community. The point of nationalism that came to be associated with the search for 'Indianness' in art and a need for affirmation of an indigenous identity in every sphere of one's existence, in fact created the space for alternate modernisms with its insistence to hark back to the roots.

This possibly led on to the question of the regional face of folk culture—the immediate roots—against which the 'Indian' themes of the Bengal school seemed remote and unsubstantial, bearing little familiarity with the masses. Having said this, it is also important to underline the fact that for all the differences Roy had with them, the opposition of the Orientalists to Academic realism, as also their insistence on capturing the 'spirit' of a painting, had ushered in a discursive environment with fruitful debates and discussions that was extremely conducive for Roy to map out his own course. Conducive, too, was the contemporary cultural–political environment for such a renewal of emphasis on the folk. In the 1920s, the research on folklore got an additional impetus with the publication of Abanindranath Tagore's *Banglar Brata*, (translated in French as *L'Alponaou les Decorations Rituelles au Bengale*, it was published in Paris at around the same time), which discussed in detail the tradition of *alpana* in Bengal. Ballads of Bengal were collected by Dineshchandra Sen and Jasimuddin on behalf of the University of Calcutta, while Gurusaday Dutta, a District Magistrate, collected specimens of folk art from all around Bengal (which later constituted the impressive collection of the Gurusaday Museum of Folk Art in Kolkata) in a bid to revive the folk art tradition.[2] Besides, Gaganendranath Tagore too had several varieties of *pats* in his collection, apart from specimens of folk toys, and that quintessentially Bengali embroidered quilt, *kantha*. Jamini Roy must have seen this collection while painting Debendranath Tagore's portrait at their ancestral home at Jorasanko, along with Sunayani Devi's folk-themed paintings. Though he

2 In *The Art of Jamini Roy and the Bengal Folk Paradigm*, Sovon Som points out certain earlier endeavours that contributed to this renewal of interest in folk culture. He mentions how Reverend James Long initiated the study of folklore by collecting native proverbs and Reverend Lalbehari Dey collected and published fairy tales from the obscure interiors of Bengal villages. Significantly, an important ethnographic study of the *patua* community and their vocation was made by Taraknath Mukherjee.

had already been familiar with the likes of such art, the honour and care with which these were collected and preserved in a culturally rich, high-brow urban home may have reinforced his interest in their abiding artistic value. In this context it would be worthwhile to note that around the world, rediscovering the expressive power of such cultures has almost always occurred at 'moments of political transformation in territorial histories',[3] and had been used as a tool for firming and defining identities.

And then in the 1920s, there was the pervasive influence of Gandhi who succeeded in connecting the village masses with the nationalist resistance against the British rule. This was, in a sense, an empowerment of the rural people who had hitherto stayed at a distance from the waves of political dissent the crest of which was ridden by a predominantly high-brow, city-based leadership. This, connected with his emphasis on the development of rural economy and cottage industry, naturally brought about a renewed social interest in the cultural value of folk art. It is difficult to say whether Roy had been aware how closely aligned his (and his father's) thoughts about the rural order were

3 Bendix, Regina F., and Galit Hasan-Rokem, ed. *A Companion to Folklore*. p. 4.

with Gandhi's vision, especially those related to rural interdependence and a self-sufficient, sustainable economy. But it can be assumed with certainty that these watershed moments of history must have subconsciously justified the direction he was poised to explore. It would also be interesting to note that the year 1921, when Roy undertook the journey around the villages of Bengal to collect specimens of folk art like *pats,* folk toys and terracotta reliefs, was also the year of culmination of Gandhi's Satyagraha, which as well involved the mobilisation of the rural masses. What may have begun as an Abanindranath-inspired quest for the roots was given substance and purpose by the Gandhian ideals. In fact, 'through the twenties both Abanindranath and Gandhiji remained with him, in his work.'[4] Nandalal Bose's engagement with rural life and various folk-art forms also involved a decentering of art from its high-brow pedestal into the space of everyday, common life, and sited the national in the regional.[5]

Rabindranath Tagore, with his rural reconstruction programmes at his ancestral zamindari at Shilaidaha

4 Roy, Pranabranjan. *Jamini Roy's Art in Retrospect.*

5 It is known that Bose and Roy did have serious differences of opinion, but Bose did invite Roy to work with him on decorations for the Lucknow Congress of 1936.

and Patisar, and later, at Sriniketan (in which he was ably assisted by Leonard Elmhirst), must have been a potent influence as well, as were the views Tagore expressed in *Palligram*, *Panchabhut* and even *Kalantar*. Roy had a deep respect for him, and for his paintings for their inherent strength and rhythm,[6] and the two had met on several occasions. That he was deeply affected by Tagore's views is borne out by the underlines and comments he added to Tagore's famous essay, 'Tapoban' which appeared in a 1316 volume of *Prabasi*. One of the sections he marked was:

'If India compels herself into subservience to European ideals, the result would be a distorted India rather than a true Europe...one has to firmly understand that to imitate and to follow cannot define the relationship between two races—it should be one of mutual give-and-take. If India cannot become pure India, then she will have no place in the world apart from laboring at someone else's market; this will result not only in the departure of self-respect, but also a loss of joy in her own existence.'

6 In Tagore's paintings, Roy located that 'lively backbone' that protested against the void that appeared in Indian painting for the previous 200-odd years, since the Rajputs.

In this Roy possibly found the clear corroboration of his own growing impatience with Western academism; it was conceptually supportive, too, of his search for an indigenous identity in art. He writes in the margins of the page: 'Today I got to see the feelings of my mind in a written form—I had arrived at this realization eight months back—18 *Jaistha*, 1330.' The year would then be 1922/23, which coincides neatly with the period when he had just finished his tour of the Bengal villages, after having collected folk art and artifacts and also having received lessons in their trade from practicing folk artists. A few years later, in 1929, he was to show to the public his first experiments with folk art.

This journey of Roy's to collect folk art can actually be seen as an aesthetic revisit to the folk forms he had been familiar with, from his very birth to early teens, in his native village at Beliatore. Folk art usually remains so deeply ingrained in rural life that it becomes a matter of habituality: it is a part of rituals, of entertainment, even day-to-day essential requirements, and thus their intrinsic artistic value is hardly noticed separately by those who are generously surrounded by their ubiquity. The figure of the artisan, who in fact can be considered as the combination of craftsman and artist, hardly ever considered art as an end in itself, but rather as something that added value to functional products. If we try to apply the standards of artistic appreciation we are familiar with now, there was indeed a kind of aesthetic invisibility about these. A general awakening of interest in folk art, typically in urban centres, led usually by urban intellectuals, brought about a change in the perception of value in folk art. If we consider the matter closely, it is really about how relocation mediates with the perception of significance: a *pat* by an anonymous *patua*, a *kaantha* sewn by a female elder of the family, wooden figurines or toys made by a carver in huge numbers to be sold to children in fairs acquire special, focused significance once they are shifted out of context and are moved to urban centres of appreciation, be it the Gurusaday museum, Gaganendranath's home or Jamini Roy's studio. And this is specifically the point that is so fascinating in Jamini Roy's engagement with the folk. It clearly has two distinctive layers: the first is the reminiscence of his younger days of being habitually surrounded by both material and non-material forms of folk culture integrally rooted to lived life, and the second is a considerably evolved engagement with these as 'art', as opposed to simply good-looking, useful, entertaining things that used to be taken for granted in an earlier period, when the delight in these remained untranslated along aesthetic lines. The latter attitude could not possibly have come about without the mediation of the intervening years and his close engagement with urban modernity. Thus he was, at the same time, an insider and an outsider to the folk idiom, both rural and urban, negotiating between a nostalgic subjectivity and an objective search for significant form. In a way, Roy was journeying between selves, between distinct modes of relationship: these coalesced in his work, recombined and grew, just as human relationships grow and transform.

As has been mentioned before, Jamini Roy had been drawn by the features of both simplicity and simplification inherent in folk culture, especially in folk art. In a way, thus, his quest was idealist and formalist at the same time. He was attracted by the extreme accessibility which could address and thus unite the entire community, through the use of familiar sets of cultural reference common to all. This could also be seen as the power of the simple, the accessible and the anonymous, which was tuned to hold together the basic pattern of common rural lifestyle in all its simplicity, unencumbered by excesses. But the chief point that attracted him was the formal simplification inherent in folk art, especially in the *pats* and the toys—a feature that simplified the lineaments of the subjects down to the bare essentials, throwing to the winds any concerns about verisimilitude while preserving the basics of recognisability. This feature of moving away from mere surface resemblance while presenting the essence in an abstracted form is the very basis of folk art, and of folk artists who were untrained in evolved academic techniques and followed the age-old conventions which had become almost formulaic. Jamini Roy marvelled at the way the ancient *pat* artists could discover what he felt was 'the final truth in art'[7], though he did maintain that this gradually became a repetitive convention, and ultimately an artistic habit of the *patuas*. Roy believed that for the earliest folk artists, the depiction of the purity of form was a conscious choice. They did not try to imitate nature, ever, but wanted to communicate 'the feeling and the vision of a mind reacting to the universals of nature.'[8] Apart from the form, Roy was also drawn by the way the *pats* were steeped in an immersive

7 Roy, Jamini. *Patua Shilpo*. p. 69.

8 De, Bishnu, and John Irwin, *Jamini Roy*. p. 111.

world of myths, which themselves thrived on layers of imaginative abstraction, yet were rooted to reality. An example would be the figure of Jatayu: it was, clearly enough, not a bird of the mortal world, yet had the basic characteristics of a bird. The same could be said about the figure of Hanumana, the mythical Monkey God, who is not the kind of monkey one would expect to find in the zoos; yet, all the zoo monkeys do share some basic characteristics with him. The *pats*' reference to this non-mortal, yet humanly apprehensible world of myths, their negotiation of recognisability and abstractedness, had a deep influence on Roy's work. This is the basis, also, on which he had differentiated between 'primitive' and folk art; he insists that primitive art, in spite of its features of simplification, did not have the cohesive universe of myths, and hence lacked the iteration of a conscious artistic truth. Prehistoric man had the desire to fix the moment, be it a hunt, a dance or a ritual, and these remained fragmentary and unrelated to each other, without a cohesive mythology which could subsume them within a pattern of culture. Keeping in mind that in India there had already been a technically mature, classical tradition of art in existence, Bengal folk painting cannot be compared to the early cave paintings and other specimens of primitive art around the world. One would guess that Roy found in the former a conscious translation of wisdom derived from nature and experience, while in primitive art the communication is intuitive, yet unconscious, like a child's vision, and hence not conducive to a pattern of knowledge.

Yet he was deeply fascinated by child art. Jamini Roy had a sizeable collection of children's drawings, including those of Bishnu Dey's daughters and his own children. He had himself confessed how the drawing of his four-year-old son Patal had shown him a fresh direction when he was struggling to break off from his older art practice. The simple wonder of the child's vision, untarnished by the visual habits of the adult, provided him with a unique manner of engaging with the world of art. In fact, according to his own admission, the wide, stretched eyes of his figures owe to the way in which his son used to draw eyes: to accommodate the perception of largeness, these often went beyond the outline of the face.

The *pats* of Bengal, with which Roy remained especially rapt (he even used to call himself a *patua*), are broadly of two types, the *jorano pat* (scrolls) and the *chouko* (square) *pat*. The former was closely connected to storytelling and the performative mode, as the *patua* used to unroll the *pat* gradually and tell the tale illustrated in stages in the scroll. He would create a verbal and visual text—what Kapila Vatsyayan calls a 'kinetic text'[9]—and his impulses were both spontaneous and simultaneous. The subjects would usually be familiar tales from myths, legends or the epics, with which the community could relate easily. The square *pat* was smaller, often painted on handmade coarse paper in the same spontaneous manner. It is important for us to remember that in Jamini Roy's works, the spontaneity of the folk painters seems to be replaced by a studied control on both his technique and subject, undergoing, what one may call an urban translation. Of further interest is the variety of the square *pats*, comparatively smaller, some of them known as *Jadupats*, originally familiar to the Santhals and also the Bediyas of erstwhile East Bengal. There indeed was some magic (*jadu*) involved in the way the *jadu-patuas* got about transacting their business. After the death of a person (usually in a

9 In her introduction to Amitabha Sengupta's book *Scroll paintings of Bengal: Art in the Village*. p. 6.

Santhal household), they would visit the bereaved family and produce a roughly made portrait of the deceased, which would be merely schematic with no attempt at verisimilitude. They would, however, leave the eyes blank, without painting the iris. Then the family would be told that the deceased is wandering about blindly in the other world, and the only way to help him would be to send him some money or other articles through the *jadu-patua*. After being paid in cash or kind, the *patua* would then draw the iris on the portrait-eye, performing the act of *chakshudaan*, literally, which is why this variety is often known as *chakshudaan-pats* as well. This curious alternation between a blank eye and a seeing eye could have been noted by Roy—after all, he had Santhals as neighbours at Beliatore. We will see, in Roy's works certain figures with eyes only in the outline, without the iris, and such paintings are numerous. There seems to be, however, no intention to indicate blindness, be it physical or spiritual; nor is there any recognisable underpinning of deeper significance in the unseeing eyes. It is possible that he remembered the images, both before and after the 'magic' transformation by the *jadu-patua*, and adopted them in his work, eliminating in the way the trails of signification these were attached to in their original context.

Even apart from the *pats*, the tradition of terracotta toys and figurines of Roy's home district Bankura are examples of such masterly simplification of form. Terracotta artifacts had been, and still are, considerably popular in Bengal, and these are localised mainly in two regions—Murshidabad and Bankura—and have widely differing characteristics. The Murshidabad earthenware products are known for their adherence to realism: fruits, food products, even insects are meticulously crafted to create the illusion of the real thing. Situated in an opposite pole are the Bankura terracotta toys and figurines. The best example would be the Panchmurha horse (familiar to many, being the symbol of the Central Cottage Industries) which has no resemblance to an actual, real-life horse, yet is recognisable as one, as the basic physical characteristics of the animal have been combined here with a stark simplification of its form. The sense of strength and erectness that we usually associate with the horse is preserved in this simplified form, along with a certain pleasure of rhythm in its solid presence. This is the tradition, that travels away from the exactness of resemblance, imaginatively reconstructs the object along essential lines, yet retains a clear recognisability—something that had surrounded him in his early days of childhood, and had trained his eye to look for the essential form in objects around him. The colour of terracotta was also one of his most favoured hues that he had frequently used in his paintings. He had also been interested in dolls, and other clay arts of different regional variations. In a letter to Debiprasad Chattopadhyay, who had been visiting Puri then, Roy had especially requested him to bring back, without fail, local handcrafted items like stone oil-lamps (*pradeep*), clay items and whatever dolls that caught his fancy.

We see the deep formal influence of the wooden/earthen animal figurines and toys particularly in the way he captures his animal motifs. Animals are frequent in Roy's work—he painted horses, tigers, elephants, bulls and cows, and numerous cats. In many of these we notice the lengthening of the body rather in the fashion of terracotta toys, where the space of the body between the pairs of legs is stretched out and the legs are shortened (as in the cows in *Krishna and Balaram*, ref. pic 03). In the untitled painting of a horse in tempera (ref. pic 08), we see the familiar form of the Bankura horse, only it involves an interesting opening up of the mass of the figure that is supposed to lie invisible behind the fully frontal face. In defiance to illusionist logic, we are shown the back and the tail. The final effect is that of two horse-bodies sharing a single face, but, interestingly, it has six legs instead of four or eight: in an enigmatic leap of experiential logic, we are allowed to confront the autonomy of aesthetic representation. In the painting of two cats sharing a prawn, the clear thematic echoes from Kalighat *pats* are all but submerged in the schematic monumentality of the effect, and also the sense of perfect symmetry in the mirror-image reduplication of the cat motif. These are cats that exist not on the plane of reality as we know it, but are remorphed into uniquely aesthetic identities within the space of imagination; only the faint narrative reminiscences as well as the streamlined forms are rooted to an earlier, remembered referentiality.

And then there was the profound influence of the *alpana*, the homespun designs drawn on floors with rice paste, using a wisp of cloth and a single finger. In Bengal the *alpana* belonged exclusively to the domain of women, and was usually connected to rituals and *bratas*. The inherent narration of cultural continuity was a feature of these household ritualistic festivals which also held fascination for the artist. The *bratas*, and the timeless tradition of the *alpana* with its meaningful motifs, were very much a part of the cohesive nature of folk culture that continued to resist external forces of disintegration. It was also, at least origin-wise, beyond the compartments of religion: we may also remind ourselves of the fact that many of the *patuas* were Muslims, who adopted the title of '*chitrakar*', privileging thus their artistic self-identity over the religious. And there was also that not-unusual phenomenon of synthesis in folklore which brought together elements from distinct religions: an example would be that of the Muslim figure of *Satya-pir* who was later appropriated as *Satya-narayan* by the Hindus (as Abanindranath points out[10], the *Satya-narayan panchali* in Bangla originally depicted the god in the garb of a Muslim). Though Roy himself was a devout Hindu, he regularly consulted the almanac, and almost all his letters began with the mention of *Sree Sree Hari*—it is the secular vitality of folk culture, and the cohesive power flowing from it, that seem to have particularly attracted him. It would be interesting to observe that most of his women, in spite of being clearly denoted as married, do not wear sindoor, or sankha-pola, the traditional signs of marriage that

10 *Banglar Brata*. p 20.

Bengali women were obligated to wear, but they do have the ghomta covering their head. In his earlier, Kalighat-inspired paintings, we have many versions of 'Woman' or 'Mother and Child'—the hair-parting is left bare, and the hands are bereft of the red/white bangles so typical of Bengali married women. We notice the same in his later works. Was he deliberately trying to remove these clear markers of religious identity, as he was addressing the community as a whole, and perhaps did not wish to deploy signs that might be read as segregational? This only further corroborates the contention that he drew not essentially from the Hindu religion, but from the myths that formed the enclosing circle of common referentiality which included the entire community, notwithstanding the differences of religion. His women are also curiously genderless—even when he is dealing with a theme like the *Vastraharan* (the snatching away of clothes) of Gopinis by Krishna, the women display no perceptible sexuality in spite of their nakedness. Perhaps eroticism was a part of that 'excess' for him which was inessential in his scheme of abbreviation, and would possibly have intervened in his social outreach.

The *alpana*, which has, somehow, been able to continue with its presence in Bengali homes even in our times, has extremely interesting formal qualities. Most of these are highly concentrated, minimalist representations of subjects belonging to the world of flora and fauna, like the leaf, the flower, birds and fish, and the functional objects of everyday usage, like the *kalash* (water-vessel), the triangular shape of the *gola* (granary) and the *saankh* (conch-shell) and of course, the symbolic footprints of the goddesses. It was assumed that if one reproduced the objective of one's prayer in a motif of images and prayed in front of it, the wish would be granted: this was probably the primary impulse behind the *alpana*, which, however, did not stop just there, but acquired artistic embellishments. It is, as if, the gap between the wish and its fulfillment in a *brata* is a space that accommodated ripples of emotion; and this is the state conducive to the birth of the artistic, the aesthetic and the effulgent that adds the pattern of beauty and harmony to the representative images in an *alpana*. In Jamini Roy's works, we find liberal use of the *alpana* motifs, especially the unbroken spiral, circular in shape, with decorative dots surrounding the circumference. The circular pattern often changes to a triangular one, with similar use of dots (as seen in *Mary and Jesus*), which may be referenced (ref. pic 10) to a granary, which signifies in Bengal a sense of plenitude and happiness. In the borders of his paintings, he often uses variations of the *lata*, a creeper with fruits and flowers, frequently used with a stylised repetitive regularity in the main body of the Bengal *alpana* or in its borders. He uses these motifs with the same minimalist approach as in the *alpanas*, and with the same conceptual mooring to nature and reality. In fact, the design of creepers drawn in this homespun art has great variety and creativity: *khunti-lata*, *chalta-lata*, *shankha-lata* are variations of the same basic design. The *shankha-lata*, with its simplified representation of the spiral of conch-shells, is even thought to have its antecedents in the folk art traditions of ancient Crete, Egypt and Greece. It is clear that Roy used the *alpana* motifs in order to utilise their function as cultural signifiers, in order to root his work specifically to the cultural history of Bengal. In that sense, he is addressing a space and people at once, and it would be a misnomer to consider his use of these motifs as having a mere decorative purpose.

The Dialect of Global Art

Roy's indebtedness to the terracotta panels in the famous temples of Bankura is usually not distinguished from folk art. But Roy himself had made the clear distinction between traditional art forms prevalent in Bengal. He subdivided these into two categories, of which the first was homespun art, or art related to day-to-day life, while the second was 'formal' art, which was connected with celebration of occasions, like that of the idols of gods and goddesses. The first category is entirely unconcerned with cosmetic perfection or correction, but the second is much more evolved and somewhat aristocratic, often rooted in the Vedas or similar traditions. He is possibly referring to the high-brow and low-brow existent even within the rural visual culture, and it will make sense if we consider the temple panels to be a part of the first category. We must remember that these famous temples with their unique 'Bengal' architecture and terracotta art were commissioned by the Malla kings of Bishnupur, and were executed by a group of highly skilled artists/artisans with hereditary knowledge and skills, depicting mostly Puranic tales on the panels. Thus it was in a different league from the naiveté and simplicity inherent in folk art, and tended more towards the classical. But here too there had been an interface with the folk tradition, as it is said that as most of the artists were unlettered, they based their interpretations of the *Puranic* stories on the retelling of these by villagers. Understandably, thus, elements of folk narratives mediated with the representation of traditional themes in the temple panels. Many paintings of Jamini Roy have the same tight composition of these panels and the themes, too, are similar in many cases. Some are frieze-like, with many characters in a single, frontal plane, clearly recalling the relief work in the terracotta tiles. But the point that is often overlooked is the way Roy's use of the cropped image can be traced to these panels. It has always been thought that his occasional use of cropping—that is, selecting only a part of the subject and indicating that there is more just beyond the field of vision—was a distinctly Western influence. Cropping in Western art was influenced by photography, and was first used by the Impressionists, whose works Roy must have been closely familiar with. But there is clearly no reason for overlooking the connection of this stylistic technique of his with the cropped images used in these temple panels, undoubtedly familiar to him, which were created centuries before it appeared in Western painting. His use of the *tribhanga* (triple-bend) stance—that is, the standing body position in which the body bends at the knee in one direction, at the hips in the opposite one, and in the other direction again at the shoulder and neck—can be traced back to his first-hand familiarity with the terracotta murals of the Bankura temples. This position, imparting a sense of rhythm and fluidity (somewhat equivalent to the contrapposto or the s-curve of Western art, though there the bends are much less emphasised), had been used in Indian art for thousands of years, including temple sculpture. In his paintings, the compromise of symmetry that such cropping could have brought about is countered by locating and establishing a 'dynamic point'[11] that reasserted balance and opened up infinite possibilities. It was possibly this rhythm that Nissim Ezekiel was thinking of, when he said that Roy made the 'spirit' of the people to 'sing and dance'.[12]

Yet it is evident that Roy's formalist interest in folk art was corroborated by the newer directions opened up by European modernist experiments in art, their emphasis on abbreviation and simplification—qualities that he could locate in folk art forms as well. The most important feature of the former was the way forms were simplified down to their geometric essentials, something that he was to firmly adopt for his own works. I would say that

11 Mitra, Asok. *Bharater Chitrakala*, Part-II. p. 131.

12 Nissim Ezekiel, in his poem 'Jamini Roy'.

his inspiration was derived almost equally from Bengal's folk tradition as well as his close brush with modernist artistic trends, operating as parallel sources because of the rather interesting equivalence between the two. Roy was familiar with the current trends and experiments of European art. He was a regular subscriber of the famous art magazine, *The Studio*, from his early days, and in his later years, numerous art journals and magazines from abroad used to arrive at his place by post. The influence of his close friend, Atul Bose, who was passionate about the new waves of Western art, must have been a formative factor as well. After Bose's return from England, he was appointed as a teacher in the Government Art School and formed the Art Rebel Centre in 1933, to counter the Bengal School ideology. Interest towards the modern art movements developed here, through their initial focus on Western Academism, not in antagonism to it, as was seen in Europe.

Roy also had a number of books on post-Impressionism and used to study them closely. His earlier technique of using patches of bright 'Fauvist' colours can be traced to the influence of Andre Derain, and in his 'pointillist' works, the separate brushstrokes are larger than those of Seurat and often tend towards divisionism.

He did feel a close kinship with Gaugin, possibly on the point of wariness with an industrial–urban society, but it was Van Gogh whose works fascinated him. Sunil Madhav Sen[13] recalls having seen a portrait of Van Gogh done by Roy, similar to the one reproduced on the cover of Irving Stone's *Lust for Life*. He copied many post-Impressionist paintings as well, in fact many of his earlier works in the post-Impressionist style were displayed in one of the rooms of his studio. The works of Picasso possibly underlined for him the need to arrive at the quintessential form. The way he treated his subjects to give precedence to purely pictorial qualities can be, with facility, seen to relate to his familiarity with Western art movements somewhat more than it did with the folk traditions. And then there was the remarkable influence of Gaganendranath Tagore, who had experimented with geometric forms, moving towards kaleidoscopic designs almost, earning thereby the label of an Indian cubist (though unlike the Western practitioners, he did not attempt structural analysis of the visuals he worked with). We may also remember the month-long Bauhaus exhibition in 1922, which included the works of Paul Klee, Kandinsky, Feininger and other prominent

13 Sen, Sunil Madhav. *Dinpanjir PataTheke*. p. 80.

members, and indicated clearly to the painters of Bengal that the practice of academic realism has ended, even in Europe. It was highly probable that the intuitive approach of the artists and the symbolic associations of colour inherent in their works resonated with Roy, who had been, by then, getting restless with working with illusionism and verisimilitude. The basic features of the Bauhaus School were, in principle, close to the quest Roy was to take up soon: its approach to design, the way it sought to combine individual artistic vision with mass production and even daily functionality was similar to what Roy would imbibe in his later art practice.

Thus Roy's veering towards the folk idiom was probably not a purely emotional decision that it is often taken to be. It was a gradual, intellectually considered process in which several essential requirements found their answer. For example, it was necessary for him to remain rooted to the culture of his land—for him this was his very own Bengal—thus the question of identity was a key factor for him. In fact he believed that in order to embed such a rooted identity, an artwork must, primarily, wear a different 'look'. In a radio interview[14] with Bishnu Dey, he emphatically stated, 'It will not be

14 Dey, Bishnu. *Jamini Roy*. p. 63.

possible for me to paint in the manner of Europe, or China, or Tibet—nor will I be able to paint like Persian or Mughal painters—only because I do not share their environment. Thus for finding my way I had to search within myself…it was my determination to make the appearance look different. Only after that would the considerations relating to its quality come about…the look creates the first impression, understanding other virtues comes later.'

It is clear that Roy, here, is thinking of identity in terms of a visual image, the representation of which is a difficult task indeed: identity does not reside in simple, visually translatable traits, but in the inaccessible recesses of consciousness, and as such can only be held together by image-metaphors. He found an approximation of this in the lines and the iconography of folk art where the characteristics of its subject is pared down to the basic minimum, with the effect that a single line, or a dab, or a curve could relate to wider visual concepts beyond itself, and yet could be understood with ease by the community. His new idiom would contain the abbreviated values of both modernism and folk art, and the pictorial surface would 'look' like the familiar images of art rooted in the villages in which even the urban could connect with their origins. The question of identity was thus inseparably connected with the question of originality, as the identity he was looking to establish was not only one of a race/religion, but of a rooted artist who had gone through an arduous process of synthesis before that unique moment of arrival.

The logical inconsistency in European religious painting was one of the points that had engaged Roy in his early days. He had interrogated the life-likeness of Raphael's *Madonna*, carrying the baby Jesus, who looked exactly like a flesh-and-blood human being, yet she was depicted as standing on the clouds. The use of light-and-shade and other tools of verisimilitude gave her body the illusion of substance and weight, which was incompatible with her position of suspension amidst the clouds. Her divine essence, Roy felt, could not be captured through such an impeccably realistic human likeness. He is clearly concerned here with the correlation of the concept with the image, the essence with the expression, and can be observed to be moving towards an alternate set of visual alphabets which would be more equipped to capture the conceptual reality rather than the apparent equivalence of appearances. In other words, he was inching towards a parallel world of aesthetic reality where the elements would pay court only to the inherent logic of the artwork, and not to the visual rules of the external world. This is the autonomous world of art, of the artist, where one does not need to pay obeisance to the accepted standards of visual reality. And this is exactly what we find in Roy's mature work, where he flattens out the space within a single pictorial plane, paying scant attention to the tools of three-dimensional illusion like volume, perspective or foreshortening. The result is the creation of a space, a world that does not, and never can, exist in reality, and that, precisely, is the power of art. It sees more than what is seen by the corporeal eye, even the shape of emotion of the individual or community/nation, and has a distinct visual language to address it. If we look closely at the painting *Mary and Jesus* (ref. pic 10), the details of both the figures and the narrative are clearly subservient to the pictorial qualities, to the 'designal' scheme on a flat plane, the geometric space division and the decorative motifs. The most interesting point to observe here is the effortless way in which Roy relocates a religious (and cultural) icon belonging to distant shores within the paradigm of Bengal's folk culture. Mary has the same wide eyes as that of Yashoda's, or the Gopis' in his *Krishnaleela*-themed paintings (as a matter of fact the eyes of his characters are almost invariably similar) and apart from her gown and cape, there is hardly anything that indicates her racial or cultural alterity. In most of his Christ-themed paintings, one comes across this unique manner of subsuming the central figure/s within the matrix of a typical rural culture of Bengal. In fact, as Jamini Roy had admitted once, these were the products of a conscious experiment: he wanted to see whether his folk idiom would work equally well with mythical elements from other cultures. In a way, then, he familiarises the culturally unfamiliar by placing it within the context of what is known and habitual, treating it almost like another addition to Bengal's repertoire of myths. In keeping with the schema of the *pats*, the importance and centrality of the figure of Mary is indicated by the size that dominates the pictorial space, while the worshippers on either side of her are diminished in stature. This is also the way in which her divinity is indicated, through the worshipping figures, who have their palms joined in a typically Indian gesture of paying obeisance to a deity. The structures with the sloping triangular roofs behind her clearly refer to the straw-thatched cottages or granaries of rural Bengal:

this, along with the *alpana* motifs, situates the moment within the familiar model of village life, and the whole painting is suffused with differing earth shades and the colour of terracotta. The motifs and the colours are signs which address both personal emotions and cultural memory, and these are utilised to indigenise icons which lose, in the process, the factor of 'otherness'.

Both memory and experience play their part in the creation/recreation of an icon, and the Christ-figure of Roy was one such: it had travelled through diverse cultural space, and recombined with elements of personal and communitarian memory. This is essentially noted in the way Christ is represented in certain works in terms of the regional perception of divinity. For example, he is often represented with raised arms and red palms (ref. pic 19 and 22), which instantly reminds us of the representation of an ecstatic Chaitanya Dev and the *Barabhoy Mudra* (gesture of reassurance), an essential feature of the divine idols in Bengal, 'thereby invoking the familiar element of devotion or *bhakti* into a religion of non-indigenous import.'[15] The bloodstained palms of Christ are transformed into the red palms all gods and goddesses in Bengal are seen to have, almost

15 Mullik, Sanjoy Kumar. *Jamini Roy*. p. 31.

without exception. It would also be interesting to note that on meeting Rabindranath Tagore in person for the first time at Allahabad, possibly around 1915–16, Roy was reminded of the Christ-figure. This meeting was like a revelation to him, which he had spoken and written about more than once:

'The room had six, seven or perhaps eight doors... Rabindranath entered the room, with a lantern of coloured glass. The same beard, the same familiar dress! As he entered, none had the power to speak. They were disoriented with wonder...that flowing robe and the lantern...Jesus Christ used to carry such a lantern. The beauty of this moment of appearance was indescribable.'[16]

Jamini Roy did indeed paint Jesus Christ with a lantern much later in his life, as a monumental, sculpturesque figure at a moment of revelatory presence. Though the figure of Christ holding a lantern had been depicted by many, including the famous *Light of the World* painted by William Holman-Hunt at around 1904 (with the lantern symbolising the light of conscience), Roy's work does curiously remind us of this early encounter with Tagore and the profound effect it had on him.

16 Dey, Bishnu. *Jamini Roy*. p. 79.

In a way, then, his Christ-themed paintings can be seen to add to the surprisingly accommodative repertoire of folk myths. But, for all his profound connections to the Bengal folk idiom, one must understand that he was in fact 'translating' the folk, even subsuming it within the matrix of an evolved artistic consciousness. He worked with folk art, but was far from a folk artist himself. One only has to look at the sophistication of composition as opposed to the naiveté of the *patua*, the studied, premeditated lines clearly different from the spontaneous lines of folk art, and the neat, even application of colour within a schema of almost geometric symmetry in place of the often playful compositions of the *pats*. In fact, he was trying to accommodate a vanishing way of life with its cohesion, simple needs and easy satisfiability within the frame of an urban culture which has travelled far from its roots. The question of this 'frame' is important not only in a cultural sense, but also on the point of the compositional architectonics of his works. Many of his paintings seem to be framed moments, still, silent and unmoving, lacking the lively animation inherent in folk art. When Roy was a student of the Government Art School, it is said that he was admonished by the Principal Percy Brown for standing at a window facing

Chowringhee instead of engaging in his task of working on a landscape. Roy is known to have replied that he was studying how the nature outside would look, framed within the window-shutters, as painting demands a boundary, a frame, really, within which the artist's vision is pictorially enclosed. This anecdote appears to be especially evocative, and perhaps symbolic, in view of the way he related to the folk in his paintings. It was, as if, he was looking at the unbroken rhythms of a life which was, even then, already becoming a thing of the past—from the position of an external viewer—framing the rural, in a sense, within an urban point of view. The inherent anxieties and even the nostalgia of an urban–industrial life served to translate the lively simplicity of the folk into a harmonious frieze where time stood still, almost a slice of alternate reality that could relate to people with its time-defying assurance.

It is this interface between the urban and the folk that is the singularity of Roy's work, and this is especially noticeable in the way he had imbibed certain features of the Kalighat *pats* particularly in his earlier works. We need to look at this category separately as it has certain distinctive characteristics that decidedly differentiated it from traditional folk *pats*: a close look is also necessary to re-assess its influence on Roy, which has been extensively, and often erroneously, commented on.

Roy had not been too enthusiastic about the authentic folk content of the Kalighat *pats*, but the fact that these had had a pervasive effect on him can hardly be debated (ref. pic 11 and 18). He was of the opinion that these were not the 'real' thing—'...their language remained rural, while their pronouncement was urban. The context and the idiom were mismatched—the paintings had fallen from their ideal.'[17] This is exactly the point that brings the fundamental process of genesis of the Kalighat *pats*, their interface of the urban and the rural, closer to the evolution of Roy's own visual language. The Kalighat paintings were an amalgamation not only of the urban and the folk, but of different strains of folk painting itself. The *patuas* who settled near Kalighat and often addressed certain city-based concerns and subjects in their paintings, came from different villages of Bengal, practicing different styles of *pat*-painting. There was, thus, already a coming together of various *pat* traditions in this community. The demand of an urban market also dictated the style and subject of the *Kalighat* painters—apart from the gods and goddesses, they also started

17 Roy, Jamini. *Patua Shilpo*. p. 91.

addressing the current urban society, often in a satirical vein. Subjects such as the Bengali *baboo* in the arms of a prostitute, or the religious guru committing adultery (as in the *Mohanto and Elokeshi* series) are seen to emerge, combining both irony and playfulness in their depiction of decadent urbanity. But this urban connect changed much more than only their subjects of treatment: it changed their technique of handling the subjects as well. While the fast, animated lines bear testimony to the necessity of completing the painting within a very short time—the faster they painted, the more they could produce, and sell—their treatment of pictorial space had also deviated considerably from the traditional *pats*, especially the scroll *pats*. Instead of the multiple figures in the latter, the Kalighat painters started favouring one or two large figures, composed with lesser space around the figures than in the village *pats*, and did away with the traditional sequence of events by replacing it with the pictorial manifestation of a single moment. This favoured their ease of execution as well as the taste of their urban clientele. While Jamini Roy did share the prolific nature of production of these painters, his lines were slower and more studied than them. He worked in tempera, not in transparent watercolour as the Kalighat *patuas*, and thus there is much less tonal variation in his works. Though his subjects never strayed away from folk life and the myths that suffused it (except for his Christ-themed paintings) he had indeed framed his 'folk' subjects within an urban sensibility, as we had discussed earlier. In this he had travelled far from the simple naiveté of the anonymous *patuas* of the Bengal countryside, and in the same way as the Kalighat painters, his art was also not so much of a 'real thing' as the traditional *pats*. And it is significant that it was not so. It is not typically the folk content, but the intersection of the urban and the rural that is fascinating about Roy's work, and much of the critical discourse about him is justifiably directed at understanding this unique synthesis.

Roy's adoption of the Kalighat 'line' in his paintings has also been subject to much critical debate. It is possible that he was initially inspired by the way Gaganendranath Tagore, to whom he had been close, had used similar free-flowing calligraphic lines in his 1921 series of lithograph caricatures, especially in the *Reform Scream* series. At around 1924, we do see Roy's use of lines akin to the Kalighat *pats*, especially in his monochrome paintings of this period, to capture the volume of his figures. But whereas these *patuas* indicated the volume and gradient through the differing tones in single fast movements of a loaded brush, darker on the outer contour and progressively lighter, bringing out instantly a semblance of curvilinear volume, Roy's technique was somewhat different. He juxtaposed a dark outer line and a grey inner one which mimicked the lines of the Kalighat *pats* (and the sense of volume these induced), but were clearly more premeditated. It was as if he was breaking up the tonally graded lines into separate colour fields, putting them next to one another, laying open to observation how the gradation of colour tones relates to the visual sense of volume. In a way, here he is playing with the tricks of three-dimensionality and the ways in which these work, exploring and exposing thus the actual architectonics of the process. This can be seen to hold cues to his actual journey towards two-dimensionality and a flat pictorial surface. It has been observed that these works lack the spontaneity of the Kalighat *pats* specifically because of the very different quality of the moving lines: one can counter-argue that it had never been Roy's intention to imitate the spirit or the technique of the Kalighat works. He did not share their world of playfulness, lighthearted satire and social judgement, and his paintings thrived by incorporating moments of stillness rather than a sense of movement. These should rather be seen as experiments in form. By separating the chromatic tones of the single, loaded Kalighat line he was possibly working on perfecting his own visual language, thus advancing towards a schematic colour arrangement and minimalism that would become his signature style in later days.

The lack of spontaneity and lively movement in Roy's lines have been the subject of much critical debate; but there is a significant component in his oeuvre that is entirely different from the schematic, *designal* premeditation noted in most of his signature works. If we look closely at his drawings and sketches, many of which were made as prior studies for paintings, it is as if we enter a completely unfamiliar world, as different as possible from the still, silent, well-wrought pictorial surface of his paintings. Technically, there is supposed to be a difference between drawings and sketches: the former is thought to be more 'finished' than the latter, done with more deliberation, while sketches are often speedy, carrying an underlying sense of the preliminary. And that is possibly why the true spirit of an artist can be traced in these. Even for the greatest of artists, an established, conventional style can impose limitations in case of full-scale artworks: but in cases of sketches, there is, almost always, the sense of an unpremeditated personal connect, free from other considerations. Jamini Roy's drawings and sketches allow us to see him in an entirely different light—not only are these free and playful and spontaneous, but these also provide us with valuable cues as to how he was progressing in his understanding of the essential form in terms of both simplicity and geometry. The lines are free and fast, with a life of their own, some of them having almost no resemblance to the lines that we encounter in his major works. In his paintings the lines enclose areas of colour—as contour lines, as definers of shape, and also as indicators of the stark simplicity of form—while in case of the sketches the lines seem to be set free from these functional exigencies. They move, and come to life, and we notice how the organic and the geometric exchange glances in these exercises with line and form. If Roy's finished paintings refer to a world of perfect rhythms and balance, these acknowledge a world that is imperfect and throbbingly human. If we compare his pen- and ink-drawing of *Mary and Jesus with Four Apostles* (ref. pic 07 and 10) with his painting *Mary and Jesus*, the difference in the character of lines becomes immediately noticeable. In the latter, the lines are more studied, more contained, while in the former the lines are freer and livelier, liberated, as it were, from subservience to a schema. These are faster here and more overlapping, and perhaps hold within themselves the passion related to the moment when a concept or an idea connects with the visual. These are also much more organic, in spite of the overarching geometric sense and the symmetry of the composition. Some drawings of his also deepen our understanding of how he arrived at his curvilinear lines in his paintings, lines which treat the figures in terms of *both* the geometric and the organic. And then there is that clear sense of abbreviation—an impulse to denude the figures down to their bare formal essentials—this minimalist quest is present equally in his sketches and drawings (ref. pic 01, 05, 06, 07) as well as in his paintings, and forms the very basis of his unique artistic idiom. Unfortunately, he would draw on any paper that he could find close to him, and this often included pieces of waste and torn papers. That is possibly why many of his drawings and sketches have not stood the test of time and could not be preserved. Otherwise, there would possibly be in existence a much larger number which then could have become a significant, and independent, subject of study, for in these we get to see certain aspects of the artist which are very different from those encountered in his major paintings.

Roy's sculptures, mostly in wood and clay, provide us with significant insights as well about the way his creative impulse actually worked. He worked on most of his wood sculptures during 1942, when he had to take refuge at his village home, Beliatore, having left Calcutta because of the scare of possible bombing. With the aid of an able carpenter, whom he referred to as *Sutradhar mistri,*[18] he completed a number of sculptures in wood, all of which bear testimony to the search for the essential form through simplification that was integral to the artist's creative journey. In these, he tried to preserve as much of the wood's original character as possible, avoiding thus any drastic reduction of the mass of the material. The human form, mostly the face, is the main subject in most of these, and the geometric, often angular planes at times tend towards the abstract with only a tenuous resemblance to any real-life antecedent. Though, according to Ajit Chakravarti, the *taille directe* (direct carving) method was more suitable to Roy's temperament, he also worked on a number of

18 Dey, Bishnu. *Jamini Roy*. p. 100.

clay sculptures which show the influence of the deep connect he had with the folk artisans' methods and products. The clay sculptures, though comparatively smaller to the wooden ones, retain the unique character of monumentality: in these, he uses the process of addition for creating ample volume. This is distinct from the process of deduction that is utilised in case of wood, where one cuts away at the material to arrive at the sculpted form.

Early in 1926/27, when Roy was still searching for a new idiom, he had brought artist Bhabesh Sanyal to his Bagbazar home, along with a lump of alluvial clay from the banks of the Ganga, which was nearby. They sat side by side, playing, as it were, with the lump, in search of meaningful forms. Sanyal understood later that Roy's search then was an early indication of the 'simplified stylization' that was to characterise his latter work; he felt that Roy's hand in sculpture was influenced by the imaginative content in the famous Bankura horse, especially the spirited strength inherent in its form.

And this is what holds close folk art and the Modernist artistic spirit: perhaps not only the simplified forms, but also the way the lines and colours hold within them the movements of the mind. It is essential for us to remember again that Jamini Roy was decidedly not a folk painter, he was well settled and comfortable in his urban moorings, and was in fact not very happy when he was necessitated to return to his native village for some months. Even if we go by the 'look', most of his well-known paintings do not resemble traditional village art. The schematic stylisation and symmetry in them completely lack the spontaneous flowing lines and the essential naiveté of the folk painters. I would call it a process of translating the folk, rather than adopting its idiom: the process is complicated, many-stranded, mediated by influences belonging to other worlds. Much has been said about his minimalism, about his abbreviated lines, but what is especially notable is how he combined these with the decorative character (also derived from folk art) to fabricate a unique pictorial surface which was redolent with cultural reminiscences of a slowly vanishing way of life. In a sense, simplified forms are incompatible with decorativeness; one speaks of essentials, the other of excess. Although the motifs that he uses from the familiar patterns of the *alpanas* have certain symbolic significance within their own context, they are empty outside it, apart from carrying a nostalgic value perhaps. And it is this association that Roy utilises, using these motifs in the borders, and even within the paintings, primarily as cues for evoking a way of life distinct from the urban experience. This life would have the power to accommodate, and pour meaning into the mythical moments he would paint. In a way, then, these are used as signs, and the decorative surface is actually a symbolic cultural narrative.

Perhaps ours is a time inherently most opportune than any to attempt a revisit to Jamini Roy's life and art, especially in the context of renewed contemporary interest in the folk, the subaltern, in the reclaiming of submerged discourses and the restructuring of cultural locations. Looking closely, these were also the concerns of Jamini Roy, working in a far-removed timeline, trying to solve his impatience with the art of his times which latched on to other climes and other times, and follow an aesthetic destination firmly bound to the folk culture of Bengal. His attempt to understand national identity in terms of regional culture—the siting of the national in the local, as it were—has also assumed a deeper significance in our own times. Our perceptions related to located identity are being constantly recalibrated—referenced to a seamless world as it appears to be, thanks to technology—and we find ourselves negotiating with questions of cultural rootedness with far more urgency and frequency than in the past. Where do regional figurations belong, in the fashioning of a national identity, or more importantly, is it at all feasible, even desirable, to configure a cultural uniformity of Indianness, where variable patterns are shiftingly inscribed in the mosaic of India?

These are the interrogations that remain silently embedded in Jamini Roy's work. To disentangle and find space for these within our contemporary critical discourses would be a task not only fascinating, but vitally essential as well.

THE PEOPLE'S ARTIST

One way of looking at Jamini Roy's engagement with folk culture would be to see it as an attempt at mainstreaming the marginal. We must remember that, after all, his artworks were directed at an almost exclusively urban clientele, who could appreciate and more importantly, afford even the moderately priced artworks he created. He was also patroned by a collective intellectual capital which could firmly and unwaveringly situate his works within the grand narrative of Indian art—most of the intellectuals who wrote influential pieces on his art were writers, academicians or social commentators, not art critics. Folk art had always been important in India, it still is, but it has always been limited by the parameters of its own category, separate and exclusive. We are comfortable with the folk artists' anonymity when we buy their artworks in handicraft fairs or camps which have become especially popular in our times, and the artists themselves have no qualms about going unnamed: but a visit to an art gallery would see us exercise a completely different set of attitudes. It is actually possible to see Jamini Roy as a figure negotiating with this complex politics of significance and value. It is the success of his idiom that managed to embed Bengal folk art (which had always belonged to the fringes) within the discourse of mainstream art history.

Considered closely, this was also a negotiation between two distinct systems of ideology. One was the way of considering art as community-centric (which is distinct from, yet distantly related to, the Marxist idea of the communitarian function of art) and naturally integrated with lived life. The second was the colonial concept of the 'glorified' artist, who was an individual set apart, with the gift of originality, each of his artworks seen as unique items of possession. It was, in a sense, a shift of focus from the community to the individual. It was not easy for a professional artist, whose entire livelihood depended upon the sale of his paintings, to entirely ignore this colonially propagated ideology, as it actually created the high-value market for art. This market, distinct from the ordinary buyers of cheap Kalighat paintings, brought into existence certain extra-artistic yardsticks of appreciation. The artist's signature, for example, got an added value further by his intellectual reception, and often rode above the artworks' aesthetic value. Jamini Roy was not unaware of how this system worked—in his early days, as a portrait painter, he had become so well known that to have a portrait painted by him was in fact fashionable, and he received numerous commissions. The system of commissions is in itself interesting, as it involves the ordering/pre-booking of an artwork not yet in existence: its value, at that point, rests entirely on the name/fame/style of the individual artist, the aesthetic value of the proposed painting already subservient to these other factors. Having passed through this phase, it was hardly possible for Roy to embrace the customary anonymity of the folk artists, for he was well aware of the logistics of the market on which his livelihood depended.

He thus had to devise a strategy that reconciled the ideology inherent in the village painters' practice with the conditions related to the marketing of artworks. It is known that he deliberately kept the price of his paintings low enough to be affordable even to the middle class, who, interestingly, had never really been buyers of art till then, though a considerable section among them had a fair idea about the art of their times through the plates of paintings that were regularly published in the popular periodicals. So in a very real sense, he was creating his own market where there was none in existence. The earlier market for his portraits and oil paintings had been mainly limited to moneyed patrons; the way he managed to create a clientele even among the middle class is significant in itself. He produced a staggering number of paintings so that the prices could be kept low, taking the help of his son Patal and his friend Mantu (Manindra Chatterjee), his daughter-in-law even, in the spirit of a workshop. Certain contemporaries sarcastically called his studio a 'factory', in which 'stacks of paintings, after production, got his sign on them, almost like thumb impressions.'[1] He had himself expressed his wish to see his paintings, instead of calendars, adorn the walls of middle-class homes (which was seen as a clever marketing ploy by some of his harshest critics), and it is entirely possible that his intention was much more than only to transform the visual culture of the Bengali domestic interior. As we had discussed earlier, he may have wished to make art an integral part of urban daily living just the way it

1 Sanyal, Bhabesh. *Kichhu Smriti*. p. 76.

was in the villages. But the most important point was the replacement of the concept of the 'rare' and valuable original with a supply of art that was affordable, and at the same time non-intimidatingly approachable both in its simplicity and familiarity of subject. In fact, Roy believed that it is essential that an artwork should not be beyond the grasp of common people, both in point of price and understanding. His house and his studio operated in tandem to the tune of art, each member of the household contributing in one way or the other to the creation of artworks, reminiscent of the way in which the entire family of folk painters participated in different aspects of production. Thus we do not really need to regress to the example of the collective nature of medieval European guilds in order to justify Roy's manner of work: we already have, close at hand, the instance of the folk painters' ways of production which continue along similar lines even today. As to the critical objections to his repetition of subjects and motifs (which was seen to compromise the exclusive singularity of his individual artworks), it can be argued that if one acknowledges his folk roots, it is only logical that one should also accept the manner of execution of the folk arts. Repetition and cheap distribution were inherent to the trade of the folk artist, and there would be no sense in rejecting it just because it provided a contested counterpoint to the 'glorified' image of the artist in an urban context. Perhaps it was Roy's way of seeing the artist as an artisan that brought about a hidden unease by mediating with colonial perceptions of the artist's elevated status, and the 'rarity' of artworks. He also located an admirable integrity in the practice of the folk artists, who were unabashed in supplying to a demand in accordance with a taste already well established, without privileging the 'aesthetic' value over the commercial.

The way Roy reconciled the folk painters' work ethic as well as the manner of production with the conditions of an emerging urban art market is a remarkable feat that deserves closer analysis than it has hitherto received. We had already discussed the interface of the urban and the folk in his paintings: we can understand now that even apart from the question of theme, technique and treatment, his very manner of execution and marketing incorporate further aspects of this interface. In a sense, his art originated from the community, and it directed itself at the community as well, though in the second instance it was one that was predominantly urban. But it remains undeniable that he had always valued the recognition and appreciation of the common people. He possibly wished to replicate in an urban context the mass appeal that the folk art forms had in the villages; in a way, a full circle would be completed then.

It was possibly a combination of all these factors that led him to be hailed by the communists as a true 'Peoples' Artist'. By the late 1930s, the left cultural movements and their efforts to take art to the people brought about newer definitions of 'progressive art'. It is said that the Communist Party of India urged him to declare himself so, but Roy was not interested in getting involved in active politics. Gopal Haldar even claimed the exclusive right of the communists over the art of Jamini Roy (in his essay '*Jamini Roy o Jatiyo Chetona*') by insisting that the rich people, travelling by cars, who frequent his exhibitions are not the true connoisseurs of his art. According to him, his art related to the national tradition which was of the people because he used the language of folk art.[2]

Austin Coates mentions an interesting anecdote in his essay 'A Peasant's Painter': 'One day, after a

---

2 In another essay, 'Culture o Communistder Daiyitto', Halder unequivocally puts forward his view that exhibitions of folk art would make the working people confident about their creative power. For a detailed discussion, see Chilika Ghosh, *Realism and the Issue of Taste: Marxist Cultural Debates in the 1940s*, p 53

Communist had been particularly importunate that Jamini Roy declare himself a "people's artist", he turned to me and said, pointing at one of his pictures, "The carpenter who made the frames. The beauty of his work". It is clear that he was turning away from a commitment that could affect both his work and his general acceptability if he publicly affiliated himself with a particular political faith: instead of explanatory words, he silently underlined through his gesture his private and intimate reverence of the handiwork of the anonymous, unremembered framer—who was not even an artist, technically. It is this sense of deep respect for the artisan that extended to include the farmer, the potter, the weaver and all those who toiled with their hands to make a living, which indicates that he had already found his commitment, one that he followed silently and without fanfare. It is perhaps true that his inherent reticence could have been incompatible with political activism, but we also need to realise that his views harboured an inherent challenge to the urban-industrial power structures to which the country was succumbing at that colonial juncture. As such it was deeply political in a very real sense, and needed neither support nor corroboration from any theoretical or functional doctrine. His idealisation of a rural–agrarian system of economy may have been a reason why his empathy towards the farmers/peasants did not extend to include the urban factory labourers who had already emerged as a visible social group in his times.

He had, however, been close to the left–liberals who were his contemporaries, and was wound up in the emergent discourses. In 1942, in a large public meeting, a committee was organised to set up the Anti-Fascist Writers' and Artists' Union to counter the destructive nature of fascism. Presided over by Ramananda Chatterjee (the editor of *Prabasi* and *Modern Review*), the meeting was attended by Roy, along with prominent liberals and Marxists of Calcutta including Abu Sayeed Aiyub, Amiya Chakraborty, Buddhadev Bose, Bishnu Dey, Hiran Sanyal and Subhash Mukhopadhyay. It was here that a leading left intellectual said that 'there is none more creative among Indian painters' than Jamini Roy.[3] We need to remember that the political potentiality of art and literature was more a matter of concern then among many progressive intellectuals, rather than actual political commitment: a reason for this could be the

---

3 Chatterjee, Ratnabali. *The Original Jamini Roy: A study in the Consumerism of Art.* p. 13.

fact that the Communist Party was itself underground from 1934 to 1942, and its mechanisms, thus, could be deployed in the cultural field only in a dispersed manner. The progressive artists and critics connected with the Parichay group—some of whom were closely associated with Roy and greatly admired his work—were also not often inclined towards active politics. The left-leaning intellectuals were more concerned with figuring out the dimensions of 'progress', building on attitudes both anti-colonial and anti-fascist, where the vision of the 'people' took on transnational connotations. They also explored potential relations between 'scopes of the modern and popular in visual art.'[4] Such attitudes often surfaced in many of their writings on Roy, while trying to examine the deep connection of his art to a living tradition of the people unsullied by colonial modernity. In fact, there is a view that despite Roy's disinterest in formal political affiliation, his vision for the future was distinctly Marxist: in an interaction with a senior official from the Russian Embassy, Roy had shared his intimate thoughts about the way life should be lived—in a state of unity despite diverse traits, working in simplicity, not

4 Sunderason, Sanjukta. *Partisan Aesthetics: Modern Art and India's Long Decolonization*. p. 47.

in conflict over luxury commodities, the relationship between people neither smothering nor distant. The official, Comrade Erzine, was fascinated to hear in his simple words the echo of their most progressive Marxist thoughts, their figurations about future society. Excited, he expressed his appreciation of Roy in a close caress, which astonished the artist.[5] He also worked on a painting of Gandhi and Rabindranath, especially commissioned for gifting to the Soviet Prime Minister, Nikolai Bulganin and Communist Party Secretary, Nikita Khruschev when they visited India in 1955: interestingly, even after finishing the artwork with a passionate burst of energy, Roy ultimately refused to hand it over. He felt that it deviated considerably from his own style; its post-impressionistic treatment, he felt, did not reach that level of excellence which would find favour in the country of destination.[6]

It has always seemed, however, that his views had more of a Gandhian underpinning to them, in his faith in the close-knit, self-sufficient village economy and his distrust of embracing a mechanised civilisation at a time

5 Dey, Bishnu. *Jamini Roy*. pp. 16–17.

6 Debabrata Roy, the artist's grandson, narrated this incident in an interview with the author.

when the country's capacity of mechanical production was still limited. We may remember how he used to press his palms to his ears whenever a plane flew over his Ballygunge residence: he believed the planes could break down any moment, as the people here merely knew how to pilot them, without knowing anything about the practical manufacture of its parts. But at that particular cultural juncture, his art, with its unique intersection of the folk and the modern, had naturally become a fit subject to be appropriated by the socialist debates of the time regarding the formal and social value of art. This, in conjunction with his methods and intentions for reaching the common people, made him a pivotal figure in the emergent left-wing cultural discourse of the times. We may recall that the Indian People's Theatre Association (IPTA) at that time had also been figuring ways in which art could be taken to the people. The collective nature of Roy's art must have had a role to play as well in his popularity to the Marxists—it was antithetical to the capitalist idea of the artist as a genius who played solo to produce 'masterpieces', beyond the grasp of the masses.

It was actually a close relational network that connected Roy with the progressive, left-leaning intellectuals of Bengal, some of whom wrote lengthy pieces on the artist. He had been associated, along with his close friend Bishnu Dey, Debiprasad Chattopadhyay and many others, with the cultural activities of the Leftist Anti-Fascist Writers' and Artists' Association. When the group decided to stage the play *Punorujjibon* to gather funds for the treatment of the ailing young poet Sukanta Bhattacharya, at around 1945, the problem they faced was with the representation of the resurrected Christ at the very climax of the play. Jamini Roy had been experimenting with the Christ myth for quite some time then and, as we had noted before, had negotiated with similar problems in representing the divine in human terms. Roy advised them to cover the figure of Christ in white cloth, from top to bottom, so that even the most minimal body movement would be invisible to the audience. He also painted a uniquely designed mask for the Christ-figure—it was grey with deep black and vermilion streaks. Debiprasad Chattopadhyay recounts[7] how, in spite of his plans to procure and keep the priceless mask after the show, Dhrubo Mitra, who played Christ, beat him to it!

---

7 Chattopadhyay, *Debiprasad. Jamini Roy: Patrabali o Prabandha.* pp. 79–80.

There had been, and still is, a critical counterpoint in existence that Roy's paintings were never really concerned with the contemporary social and political upheavals: he lived through two world wars, the nationalist struggle for freedom, and then the famine and partition of the country, and none of these seemed to leave any significant impression upon his art. Even the fact that the source of his inspiration, the Bengal villages and the villagers, were facing rapid change in their organisation and lifestyle seemed to go unregistered, and neither his style nor his subjects responded in any significant way to such changes. This is indeed a veiled interrogation of his sustained social commitment, and an instance of a rather typecast expectation of homogeneity in artistic response. While it is true that in Roy's work there is none of the portrayal of reality or concerted social protest which, for example, we get to see in some of the works of the Calcutta Group artists of the 1940s, it is also equally true that each artist responds differently to his times and shapes his own distinct narrative. It is unjust to latch on to a preconceived notional trend of correctness and use it as a yardstick to measure deviations, as if from a pre-ordained norm. The landscapes of his earlier days portray stretches of the arid meadows of Bankura, the undulating stony fields of the Santhal homeland, women sowing seeds and farmers ploughing in the paddy fields—the atmospheric ambience that had been real to him till a certain age. Bishnu Dey mentions how he had painted urban spaces too, as he saw them around him—slums, the sad, serpentine lanes of Calcutta with its overload of closely packed houses, even loaded boats on the Ganga at Bagbazar. But there is indeed almost no instance of violence or conflict in the choice of his themes, or even in his treatment, unless we consider the curious emptiness in some of his paintings of the unmanned Calcutta streets as a trope for the de-humanising effect of an urban-industrial civilisation. There is the instance of a painting of an Indian revolutionary being snatched away by the British Police which is, however, curiously devoid of expression[8]. W.G. Archer traced qualities of independence and defiance in his treatment of the Santhals, and interestingly, also in his choice of the Christ theme. Roy's moving away from the curvilinearity of the Kalighat paintings towards a more angular style with a stress on the vertical and the rigid (like the works with dancing and drumming Santals of 1934) and the 'callous

8 Som, Sovon. *Jamini Royer Chhobi: Riti o Tatporjo*. p. 95.

disdain'[9] of their expression was ascribed to the situation arising after the Viceroy's offer of Dominion Status to India was rejected, and the years of militant action that followed. In Jamini Roy's paintings of cats with prawn or fish in their mouth (ref. pic 09) (itself a satirical theme with direct links with Kalighat *pats*), he even found echoes of the Bengali youths' longing to exterminate the foreigner: this view, however, does appear to be far-fetched indeed.

It does seem that with his folk-inspired idiom, he was trying to create an aesthetic reality which was not parallel, but actively contradictory to the fractured experience of the present which effectively rewrote the connections between the individual, the community and culture. In the face of such strong forces of transformation and disintegration, Jamini Roy's works encoded a deeper reality beyond the temporally real; these brought about a world of reassuring continuity rooted in the collective lived lives of the people and the unifying folk culture, something that had defied multiple forces of change before, and had the quiet, unassuming power to do so even in those deeply troubled times. And there was, above all, that impersonal aesthetic space with

9 Archer, W.G. *India and Modern Art.* p. 110.

its delight of lines, colours and composition which was not contingent on reality and hence inalienable from the principle of pleasure. The sense of perfect symmetry that Roy created in his paintings also puts forward a frame of reassurance in the face of dissonance and discordance: it is, as if, the beauty of the rhythms and symmetry holds together a slice of frozen time that is almost prelapsarian in its simplicity, untarnished by the forces of change. It was possibly this charmed circle that he could create in his works that made for his immense popularity. It was a space one could refer back to amid the fretfulness of the present: it would remain ever unchanging, holding the conviction that the basic regular rhythms of life do not essentially change in spite of the rise and fall in the fortunes of nations and civilisations. These are, in fact, invincible and re-assertive, with an understated power that Roy could fully utilise in his works.

Folk culture itself can be seen to possess an inherent underline of protest. Through the ages it has resisted the influx of high-brow cultures and beliefs and preserved itself against any organised cultural imposition. And it is this concerted, unified protest, repeating itself again and again in history, that has fortified it with an intrinsic strength and power that often remains undetected behind the apparent simplicity of folk culture. When an artist draws inspiration from the folk, in a sense he is utilising this inherent strength of identity and the power of resistance, and the artworks thus created, notwithstanding their apparent placidity, are underpinned by such attitudes of reassertion and resistance. We may remind ourselves of those extremely interesting variants of *pats*—the *Saheb pat* and the *Santhal Bidroho pat*—which grow around the very theme of resistance in a colonial context. These shift the focus from divine intervention as an answer to human plight, as frequently seen in mythical narratives, to human will and effort. Connected directly to the moments of resistance in lived life, these create a different order of heroic mythmaking.

In their seminal essay on Jamini Roy, Bishnu Dey and John Irwin connect several instances of social/religious revolts with the genesis of the essential character of folk culture, especially democratic mystic movements like the *Bhakti* cult which found its strongest support in and around Bankura, the home district of Jamini Roy. The folk culture came to share the movements' character of protest by defying the upper-class ethic, accompanied, however, by a rich humanism, concentrating on, as it were, 'the sensuous appreciation of life as something to be accepted and enjoyed, in marked contrast to the orthodox emphasis on prayer and speculation.' Jamini Roy captures such simple celebrations of life in the folk rituals, festivals, in the known climactic moments of myths and other familiar folk narratives: in these there is a clear underpinning of conservation and continuity, the other face of which is resistance.

The culture of simplicity was embedded in the artist's lifestyle as well, notwithstanding his financial state. Roy had never deviated from his basic, simple lifestyle even when he was at the height of his popularity and his paintings were selling extremely well. In the 1940s, the steady influx of the British–American soldiers, foreign statesmen and other overseas visitors, many of whom became ardent admirers of the artist's work, made for a phenomenally increased demand for his paintings. But even then, he is known to have resisted any augmentation to his basic cost of living: 'I have not increased my spending by a single paisa', he is known to have confided to Buddhadev Bose, who had talked at length about how, for decades, the artist's lifestyle, the look of his household, had not changed at all. It had been the same even when he had faced acute financial hardships in his earlier days—when he had to tear off sections from his own dhoti and his wife's saree to serve as a canvas for his paintings, and had to go without evening meals in order to save money to buy paints; the children were fed 'puffed rice worth a paisa' when they went hungry. His resistance to luxury and extravagance points at a distinct philosophical attitude to life which is fundamentally connected not only to his preferred lifestyle but also to his art. This is possibly why Austin Coates felt that his personality 'conveyed to an intense degree the dignity of human *suffering*'. Words are culturally contextual, often without universal referentiality—what is 'suffering' for the Western eye is, for us, simply a basic, unadorned lifestyle which fulfilled the fundamental needs of most Indian households in an earlier epoch. We must also remember that at this point, his frugality was not contingent on external factors, but self-chosen, and as such was not suffering really.

There was also a certain moderation about his habits that perfectly matched his non-exuberant personality; tea and cigarettes, that too in a limited amount, were his only excesses. He was also partial to the sugarcane jaggery that used to be one of the staples of most village households. His daily life was subject to a simple, streamlined routine that he adhered to strictly—the meals had their fixed times, after 5 pm he used to leave his studio and come upstairs to spend time with his family, while sketching on the side. His bedtime never crossed 9 pm. It would be perhaps futile to try to find any trace of the romantic in him—there was hardly any excess, any impulsive exuberance—he is not even known to have taken a travel vacation out of Calcutta, ever (apart from visits to his home-village Beliatore). He believed that Bengalis are quintessentially householders, and he himself was a perfect example of one. The minimalism, discipline and symmetry that are so closely allied to his art had formed the essential bedrock of his lifestyle as well.

His unadorned lifestyle may have had something to do with his *Vaishnavite* leanings, and the creed's principles of simplicity, renunciation and the ultimate inconsequentiality of self-regard. In fact, critics went so far as to interpret his repetition of the same motifs, forms and elements in terms of a religious incantation. The logic was that, just as chants are oft-repeated without any loss to their original power, in the same manner the energy inherent in the powerfully concentrated forms gets stronger and more socially effective through their repeated appearance.[10] His subjects are often drawn from Hindu religious myths, but almost always treated as humans, subsumed within the relational values of Bengali village life. He paints Shiv, Durga and Ganesh in the structure of a close-knit family, Krishna is an eager kid who asks for butter from Yashoda during her *dadhi-manthan* (churning of curd), *Ganesh-Janani* (ref. pic 14) resembles the quintessentially proud mother who is fulfilled by the son on her lap. Seeing the divine as human, often with multiple imperfections, is a feature of the mythical imagination of Bengal, which has succeeded in turning the traditional, all-powerful Maheswar into the *Buro-shib* who has a mean paunch, is addicted to *ganja*, and is always at the receiving end of admonitions from his wife, Durga, who has to run the family single-handedly. Durga, in Bengal, is more favoured as Uma—she is seen as a daughter who visits her father's home once a year in autumn during Durga Puja, and there is a wealth of Bengali *agamani* and *bijoya* songs which connect her arrival and departure with the happiness and desolation of real-life mothers who get to see their married daughters only for a brief period. In a

10 Asok Mitra, in *Bharater Chitrakala*, (p. 134) refers to Prithwish Niyogi's opinions on this point.

way, Jamini Roy draws not so much from the religion itself as he does from the social distillation of religious narratives, from the patterns of abiding emotional history that go far beyond traditional religious practices.

Yet he was seen by many, in his own times and later, as a 'martyr to his own mastery',[11] an artist for whom the success of a stylistic idiom effectively blocked subsequent growth and the possibility of any further development along fresh lines. It is possible that after a certain point of time, it was the market that became a significant player, demanding works of a certain style, dealing with certain subjects, thus enclosing the artist within the perimeter of an already-achieved landmark. Though we had seen him experimenting with different kinds of support like the palm-leaf matting with its woven squares, which imparted not only texture to his works but also introduced interesting geometric interplay, his subjects and the treatment of these did not essentially change. Or else we could have expected to encounter newer urban myths in his works, or explorations of how strands of the folk had consistently negotiated with the encroachment of the urban–industrial visual culture and fabricated interesting

11 Dey, Bishnu, and John Irwin. *Jamini Roy*. p. 126.

narratives of synthesis. The symmetry and the perfectly wrought pictorial surface of his paintings often remain distant from inspirational moments of epiphany, the beauty of the visuals often waylay the eye into missing a deeper vision. The tranquil harmony of his work effectively submerges the unrest connected with an inspirational flight; there is indeed some justification in seeing the 'hesitant visionary'[12] in him.

It is indeed a matter of regret how the impact of his work on the future generations of Indian artists has been limitedly appreciated, often downright nullified. When Roy's influence is seen to be confined merely to the work of minor illustrators and textile design,[13] something is clearly amiss with the way one is able to relate to the deep structure of his oeuvre as a whole. Perhaps this block in critical receptivity lies in the very appearance of the pictorial surface—the balance of colours, the geometric schema and above all, the symmetry and perfection. The allure of these persuades us to see the painting primarily as a design, and distracts us from the recognition and appreciation of the unique aesthetic space he manages

---

12 Roy, Pranab Ranjan. *Sketches of Jamini Roy*. p. 34.

13 Appasamy, Jaya. *Abanindranath Tagore and the Art of his Times*. p. 102.

to create with pure forms and symphonic colours. Even if we primarily see his paintings as 'designal', that hardly indicates a fall from the quality of a valid artwork. We must remember that design and decoration are integral to the practice of folk art just as much as simplification of forms and symbol-formation. This art-historical attitude of considering design as something not quite of the same stature as 'art' is unconsciously conditioned by the same set of capitalist ideals that had posited value in the glorified individual artist and his rare artwork, as against anonymous and communitarian folk art. The Bauhaus School had adopted design as one of their chief concerns many decades ago—Tagore's Kala Bhavan, too, had recognised its importance right from the early days of the institution. So the dismissal of Roy's work for its designal quality, even apart from its questionable critical acuity, is also historically regressive. And while it is true that textile design has indeed adopted Jamini Roy's stylised motifs, especially in Bengal sarees, as also the *Sahaj Path* illustrations of Nandalal Bose in recent times, there is nothing cringeworthy in it, unless these are bad reproductions. If anything, these bear additional testimony to his popular appeal, which had been a vitally important factor for him.

This is the exact problem that meddles with our understanding of his legacy among the later generations of Indian artists, and even his junior contemporaries. What we primarily remember is the impression of his remarkable and stylised image-combinations, and if we try and search for such a style in posterity, there would be almost no successor—except, perhaps, the works of K. Sreenivasulu, the 1923-born artist of the Madras Group, some of whose works have distinct reminiscences of Jamini Roy's style, especially in their use of cursive lines, the compositional schema and a veering towards decorativeness. We may also remember the works of Sultan Ali, whose use of elongated eyes and puppet-like faces speaks of the inspiration he drew from folk art. In fact, Ali undertook a journey to Bastar to familiarise himself with the nuances of tribal culture—something Roy had done in the 1920s to intimately understand the Bengal *patua's* art—but there were indeed differences in the way Roy and Ali interpreted the folk in their work, as can be justifiably expected.

But our search for recognisable echoes of his style obliterates the need to explore the less apparent ways in which the spirit of his works, as also the pattern of artistic attitudes inherent in them, had significantly influenced the following generations of artists. Paritosh Sen had pointed out how Roy's form-orientedness, his free use of non-local colour in certain instances—both of which, he believed, were allied to modernist art movements in the West—had deeply attracted and inspired the Calcutta group artists. In their search for a bold visual language for social protest, they were looking at formal innovations: at that juncture they, too, had been looking at folk traditions on the one hand and the newer artistic values of modernist French art on the other, and sought to combine the two intellectually. Though their work was far removed from Roy's concerns with decorativeness, his experiments with form and rejection of illusionist reality in art, as also his concern with both the conceptual as well as the optic value of the object he painted, made him inspirational to the group. The strong, erect forms in Roy's wood sculptures, which, according to Sen, were allied both to varieties of tribal art of various nation-cultures as well as the works of European avant-garde sculptors, were also significant inspirational sources. It has been observed that Roy's adaptation of the Kalighat contours had been employed by painters like Rathin Moitra, Pran Krishna Pal and Sudhir Khastagir to impart specific social and political messages through their work: instead of the 'undiluted' Kalighat contour with its attendant sensuality, they used 'its sophisticated version as developed by Jamini Roy',[14] fine-tuning the lines almost in the calligraphic mode. We sense a connecting line with Roy's work in the paintings of Ramananda Bandyopadhyay and Lalu Prasad Shaw as well, though both of them went on to shape their own trajectories through the development of distinct and individual visual idioms.

The essential dialectic in folk art, in fact in folk culture too, is tied up to the manner in which it reconciles the world of experience, in all its tangibility and *presentness*, with the space of fantasy and imagination. We have seen both these poles at work in Jamini Roy's paintings, as also in certain other significant artists of post-Independence India. The deep impress of Roy can be particularly felt in the paintings of Ganesh Pyne, who considered him to be the first ever professional artist of India in the proper sense. Pyne, in his book, reflects on Roy's work: 'At first sight his paintings seem to be mines of beauty and grace...a closer look reveals that

14 Kessar, Urmi. *A Conceptual Reappraisal of the Paintings of Jamini Roy: Analysis and Evaluation*. p. 49.

there is an ancient silence embedded in these.'[15] Here it seems as if Pyne is referring to his own paintings, to the still silent revelatory moment that these harbour deep within. Many of his works borrow their themes from ancient Bengal folklore, especially the tales of the old boatmen, and in these he weaves a magical reality which is referenced to the experiential world, yet is free from the rational bounds of reality. Often his characters, both human and animal, are endowed with many-layered symbolism and offer an instinctual aesthetic experience. It is in the intuitive creation of this ambience that he differs from Roy: there is indeed some truth in the critical view that Ganesh Pyne began where Jamini Roy left off, gathering the threads of the latter to weave magical tales of immense possibility.

Modern Indian art has drawn from the trajectory of the Indian folk tradition in several distinct ways, with artists negotiating with regional variations of folk art in their own individual manners and style. It would be unwise to bring all these lines of work, bearing variant directionalities, under a single umbrella discourse—Madhvi Parikh's assimilation of Gujarat's folk arts, for example, is very different from the way M. F. Husain

15 Pyne, Ganesh. *Swechchhay Tini Sroter Biporite*. p 227.

blended the folk and the mythological in many of his paintings. The need to define identity at a crucial colonial juncture that brought Roy close to his folk roots had continued to be a significant underpinning in case of postcolonial artistic attitudes as well, and the fact that it all started with Jamini Roy is practically undeniable. It was Roy's work which embedded the folk within India's mainstream art history (and not Sunayani Devi's folk-themed paintings, in spite of predating Roy's) because of its folk–modernist intersection which assimilated within itself those plural lines of exploration that had shaped most creative and critical discourses in his times. While this unique assimilatory aspect impressed the intellectuals with its deeper structure of thought, his paintings appealed to the middle class as well because of their accessibility in terms of both price and simplicity. The result was a wide acceptance to most sections of society which is unparalleled in Indian art history, the trail of which continues even in our own times.

In a way, Jamini Roy's career reflects the pursuits of an entire generation of artists. He had achieved proficiency in academic naturalism, which was considerably popular in his times, and were friends with both Hemen Mazumdar and Atul Bose who were unquestionable masters in this field. He had also worked in the fashion of the Orientalists, using the Abanindranath-inspired wash technique as well as the diffused atmospherics so connected to the Bengal school. This camp too had received much critical acclaim, attracting a long line of practitioners, possibly because of the nationalist concerns with which their art came to be inextricably connected. Although in time he turned away from both these then-opposed camps, he had worked along both the lines in order to work out for himself the limitations of each, before negating them and moving on to develop his singular visual idiom. He was also one of the earliest artists to understand the deep significance of the modernist experiments in Western art, at a time when the artists around him were either still following academism (which was as good as dead in the West), or looking for inspiration in ancient Indian art to cultivate a rather artificial category of Indianness. His experiments in the post-impressionist manner, especially his pointillist landscapes, show his early awareness of the value of essential forms and the power of colour, especially of vivid, non-local colours. These work wonderfully to take us back to that extremely sensitive period when tentative personal negotiation with the fresh values of modernist art were taken up by Indian artists—we remember how Gaganendranath and Rabindranath Tagore had both been deeply influenced by the spirit of Western modernism—and also the West-influenced experiments of the Bombay Progressives and the Calcutta Group, though at that time these were decades away in the future. The folk idiom, which ultimately defined Roy's identity, had also found space in the works of both Nandalal Bose and Abanindranath Tagore (in his *Krishnamangal* series, especially).

It is not only that most of the artistic concerns of the age can be traced in his trajectory: many of the contemporary aesthetic debates can actually be identified in the complex patterns of affirmation and negation in his long career, reflecting the very dialectics of an age complete with all the emergent directionalities and attitudes. In a sense, his career holds within itself the historical-discursive imprints of that most significant generation of artists and their struggles to emerge from the long shadow of the colony.

Art movements, closer to our own times, have drastically altered the ways in which we relate to art, or connect to the visual culture around us: such a change has also brought about a need to re-engage with the fixity of art-historical formulations and interrogate their assumptions of finality. Now when we look back at Jamini Roy's work after the space of several decades, we are surprised to recognise in his art practice a number of features that have been shaping not only our ways of seeing, but also a significant body of contemporary cultural discourses in our own times. The way our times have seen the breakdown of the boundaries between 'high' art and popular culture, have initiated and patronised interrogations about cultural hierarchies and the expanding significance of the peripheries, instantly remind us of Roy, as does the notion that all visual culture has equal validity and can be appreciated even without any specialised aesthetic training. Roy's thoughts far predated the postmodernist tendency to undermine concepts of authenticity and originality: he was far in advance of his times, though in a quiet and unassuming manner. We must appreciate how difficult it was for him at that juncture to de-structure the colonially disseminated construction of the 'glorified' artist, creating 'rare' artworks, and break down the veneer of inaccessibility—democratising, thus, the very process of art collection. It is indeed ironic to see how his low-priced paintings had skyrocketed in price after his demise: the collectors of these have scant interest in his idealist resistance to the received notion of 'originality', and instead, invest primarily on the basis of the signature's value. The significance of possession is reinstated again, which leaves the ideological core of the artworks practically vacant. It is curious how the reality of market dynamics and habits of art collection have an equanimous way of resisting both idealism and ideology that are premised on variance. These have value-added Roy's paintings with overtones of alterity of a past culture, relics almost, of a past way of life.

Though his dubious stand about the industrial 'progress' of India was not received too genially even by his intellectual circle, later the world did get to question whether all progress, especially technological, can actually be called positive. His art practice, centered on what was sarcastically called a 'factory', churning out artworks, is uncannily close to the concept of the collaborative nature of art that postmodern cultural theories consider significant. And that is why not only his paintings, but the nature of his art practices, deserve an intimate and rewarding revisit.

TIMELINE

15 April 1887: Jamini Roy is born to Ramtaran and Nagendrabala Roy at Beliatore village of Bankura district

1903: Joined the Government School of Art and Craft, Calcutta

1915/16: Worked at the Indian Press in Allahabad

1916: Left Art School; career as a portrait painter takes off

1919: Gets associated with Indian Art Academy, founded by Hemen Mazumdar

1920: The first issue of the journal of the Indian Art Academy publishes one of his earliest paintings on the Santhals, *A Divine Moment*; subsequent issues carry plates of his works inspired by the Bengal School

1921: Becomes Honorary Secretary of the newly formed Society of Fine Art, with Bhabani Charan Laha as the treasurer

1921–22: Goes on a tour of Bengal villages to collect specimens of folk art

1923–24: Experiments with monochromatic folk-themed paintings, in grey and brown, showing considerable influence of the Kalighat *pats*

1929: Exhibition at the Government School of Art, showing folk-themed paintings for the first time

1930: Exhibition at the Indian Society of Oriental Art, marking his complete transition to 'robust primitivism'

1931: Exhibition at his residence in Ananda Chatterjee Lane, reviewed by Shanta Devi in *Prabasi*

1935: Exhibition at the Academy of Fine Arts, received accolades for his *Santhal and Child*

1936: Decorated the venue of the Lucknow Session of Congress with Nandalal Bose

1937: Exhibition at the Indian Society of Oriental Art inaugurated by the chief minister of Bengal, A.K. Fajlul Haq; publication of Shahid Suhrawardy's essay 'The Art of Jamini Roy'

1938: Exhibition at sculptor Kshitish Chandra Roy's studio at British Indian Street

1940: Completed the *Ramayana* series for K.C. Das; this consisted of 17 large paintings

1942: Hailed as the 'People's Artist'; shifts temporarily to Beliatore to escape the threat of bombing on Calcutta

1944: Exhibition at Indian Society of Oriental Art; publication of Bishnu Dey and John Irwin's influential essay, 'Jamini Roy'; Mary Milford's essay 'A Modern Primitive' published in London in the journal *Horizon*

1946: Exhibition organised by the India Society at the Arcade Gallery in London, inaugurated by E.M. Forster

1949: Shifts to self-designed house at Dihi Sreerampore Road (later Ballygunge Place East) from rented accommodation at Ananda Chatterjee Street

1953: Exhibition at New York

1955: Honoured with Padma Bhushan

1956: Elected a fellow of Lalit Kala Akademi; *Krishna and the Gopis* shown in the exhibition of Steuben Glass, 'Asian Artists in Crystal' held at the National Gallery of Art in Washington DC

1957: Exhibited in the Smithsonian Institution Travelling Exhibition; one of the venues of the show was the Columbus Museum of Arts and Crafts in Ohio

1967: Honorary D.Litt conferred by Rabindra Bharati University

1971: Exhibition at the University of Florida Art Gallery, curated by Roy Craven

1972: Died on 24 April 1972, aged 85

1976: Government of India declares Jamini Roy's artworks as 'National Treasure'

REFERENCES

Anand, Mulk Raj. 1987. 'Jamini Roy'. *Jamini Roy Centenary Volume*. Kolkata: Jamini Roy Birth Centenary Celebration Committee. 44–49.

Appasamy, Jaya. 1968. 'Jamini Roy'. In *Abanindranath Tagore and the Art of his Times*. New Delhi: Lalit Kala Akademi. 99–102.

Archer, W G. 1959. 'Art and the Primitive: Jamini Roy'. In *India and Modern Art*. London: George Allen and Unwin Ltd. 100–115.

Bendix, Regina F., and Galit Hasan-Rokem. 2014. *A Companion to Folklore*. Chichester: Wiley Blackwell.

Benjamin, Walter. 1968. 'The Work of Art in the Age of Mechanical Reproduction'. In *Illuminations*. New York: Schocken Books. 217–251.

Bhattacharya, Ashok. 1994. *Banglar Chitrakala*. Kolkata: Paschimbanga Bangla Academy.

Bose, Atul. 1993. *Banglay Chitrakala o Rajnitir Eksho Bochhor*. Kolkata: Ananda Publishers Private Limited.

Bose, Atul. 2005. 'Jamini Roy'. In *Rupatapas Jamini Roy*, ed. Prasanta Daw. Kolkata: Pratibhash. 59–71.

Bose, Buddhadev. 2005. 'Dhanya Jamini Roy'. In *Rupatapas Jamini Roy*, ed. Prasanta Daw. Kolkata: Pratibhash. 113–122.

Brown, Rebecca M. 2009. *Art for a Modern India, 1947–1980*. Durham & London: Duke University Press.

Chakravarti, Ajit. 1992. 'Sculptures of Jamini Roy'. In *Seminar Papers: Jamini Roy*. New Delhi: Lalit Kala Academi. 13–24.

Chatterjee, Ratnabali. 1987. 'The Original Jamini Roy: A Study in the Consumerism of Art'. In *Social Scientist*, Vol 15, No 1. 3–18. https://www.jstor.org/stable/3517398 . Last accessed on 5.10.2020.

Chatterjee, Ratnabali.1990. *From the Karkhana to the Studio: A Study in the Changing Social Roles of Patron and Artists in Bengal.* New Delhi: Books and Books.

Chattopadhyay, Debiprasad, ed. 2017. *Jamini Roy: Patrabali o Prabandha.* Kolkata: Anushtup.

Coates, Austin. 1987. 'The Peasant Painter'. *Jamini Roy Centenary Volume.* Kolkata: Jamini Roy Birth Centenary Celebration Committee. 50–51.

Datta, Ella. 2013. *Jamini Roy; Journey to the Roots.* New Delhi: National Gallery of Modern Art.

Datta, Meenakshi. 1990/1991. 'The Popular Art of Jamini Roy: Reminiscences'. In *India International Centre Quarterly*, Vol 17, No 3/ 4, The Calcutta Psyche, Winter 1990/1991. 281-290. https://www.jstor.org/stable/23002469?seq=1. Last accessed on 5. 10. 2020.

Daw, Prasanta, ed. 2005. *Rupatapas Jamini Roy.* Kolkata: Pratibhash.

Daw, Prasanta, ed. 2019. *Line and Artist: An Assessment of Jamini Roy.* Kolkata: M C Sarkar and Sons Private Limited.

Devi, Shanta. 1932. 'Shilpi Srijukto Jamini Royer Pradarshani'. In *Prabasi*, Vol.32, part-1, April 1932. 127–132.

Dey, Bishnu and Irwin, John. 1944. 'Jamini Roy'. In *The Journal of the Indian Society of Oriental Art*, Vol-XII. 99–128.

Dey, Bishnu. 1987. *Jamini Roy.* Kolkata: Pratibhash.

Dutt, Gurusaday. 1990. *Folk Arts and Crafts of Bengal: The Collected Papers.* Calcutta: Seagull Books.

Dutta, Sudhindranath. 2005. 'Jamini Roy'. In *Rupatapas Jamini Roy,* ed. Prasanta Daw. Kolkata: Pratibhash. 156–178.

Ghosh, Chilika. 2013. 'Realism and the Issue of Taste: Marxist Cultural Debates in the 1940s'. In *Social Scientist*, March–April 2013,

Vol 41 No 3/ 4. 49-64. https://www.jstor.org/stable/23610471. Last accessed on 10.10.2020.

Ghosh, Mrinal. 2001. '*Grohone-borjone* Jamini Roy'. In *Ei Somoyer Chhobi*. Kolkata: Pratikshan Publications Private Limited: 59–75.

Guha, Naresh. 2015. *Jamini Roy: Ek Adhunik Chitrakar*. Ed. Prabhat Kumar Das. Kolkata: Lalmati Prakashan.

Guha-Thakurta, Tapati. 2005. 'Lineages of the Modern in Indian Art: The Making of a National History'. *In Culture and the Making of Identity in Contemporary India*, Eds. Kamala Ganesh, Usha Thakkar. New Delhi: Sage Publications. 71–107.

Gupta, Radhaprasad. 1987. '*Jamini Royer Shilper Utso Sondhane*'. In *Desh*, April, 1987. 31–34.

Italiaander, Rolf. 1987. 'Meeting with a Great Master'. *Jamini Roy Centenary Volume*. Kolkata: Jamini Roy Birth Centenary Celebration Committee. 42-23

Kessar, Urmi. 1992. 'A Conceptual Reappraisal of the Painting of Jamini Roy'. In *Seminar Papers: Jamini Roy*. New Delhi: Lalit Kala Academi. 49–68.

Krishna Chaitanya. 1994. *A History of Indian Painting: The Modern Period*. New Delhi: Abhinav Publications.

Leyden, R V. 1987. 'Jamini Roy'. *Jamini Roy Centenary Volume*. Kolkata: Jamini Roy Birth Centenary Celebration Committee. 37–39.

Mallik, Sanjoy Kumar. 2014. *Jamini Roy*. Kolkata: Rajya Charukala Parshad.

Milford, Mary. 1944. 'A Modern Primitive'. In *Horizon* x/59, November 1944. 338–342.

Mitra, Asok. 2007. 'Jamini Roy'. In *Bharater Chitrakala, Part II*. Kolkata: Ananda Publishers Private Limited: 127–136.

Mitter, Partha. 2007. 'Jamini Roy and Art for the Community'. In *The Triumph of Modernism; India's Artists and the Avant-garde*, 1922–1947. New Delhi: Oxford University Press: 100–122.

Mookerji, Ajit. 1946. *Folk Art of Bengal: A Study of an Art For, and Of, the People*. Calcutta: Calcutta University.

Mukhopadhyay, Binode Behari. 1987. 'Shilpi Jamini Roy.' In *Desh*, April, 1987. 29-30.

Pyne, Ganesh. 2005. 'Swechchhay Tini Sroter Biporite'. In *Rupatapas Jamini Roy*, ed. Prasanta Daw. Kolkata: Pratibhash. 227–230.

Ray, Pranab Ranjan. 1987. *'Jamini Royer Chhobir Thikana'*. In *Desh*, April, 1987. 39–45.

Ray, Pranab Ranjan. 2010. 'Jamini Roy's Conviction and Marketing Strategy'. In *ArtEtc News and Views*, May 2010.

Ray, Pranab Ranjan. 2012. 'Jamini Roy's Art in Retrospect'. In *ArtEtc News and Views*, July 2012.

Ray, Pranab Ranjan. 2019. 'Sketch by Jamini Roy'. In *Line and Artist: An Assessment of Jamini Roy*, ed Prasanta Daw. Kolkata: M C Sarkar and Sons Private Limited. 27–34.

Santra, Tarapada. 2011. *Folk Arts of West Bengal and the Artist Community*. Translated by Shankar Sen. New Delhi: Niyogi Books.

Sanyal, Bhabesh. 2005. 'Kichhu Smriti'. In *Rupatapas Jamini Roy*, ed. Prasanta Daw. Kolkata: Pratibhash. 76–78.

Sarkar, Kamal. 1984. *Bharater Bhaskar o Chitrashilpi*. Kolkata: Jogamaya Prakashani.

Sen, Paritosh. 1987. *'Jamini Royer Chitrakala'*. In *Desh*, April, 1987. 19–28.

Sen, Paritosh. 2005. 'Jamini Roy Ebong Calcutta Group'. In *Rupatapas Jamini Roy*, ed. Prasanta Daw. Kolkata: Pratibhash. 221–226.

Sen, Sunil Madhav. 2005. '*Dinpanjir Pata Theke*'. In *Rupatapas Jamini Roy*, ed. Prasanta Daw. Kolkata: Pratibhash. 79–81.

Sen Gupta, Amitabh. 2012. *Scroll Paintings of Bengal: Art in the Village*. Bloomington: Authorhouse.

Som, Sovon. 1982. 'Jamini Royer Chhobi: Riti o Tatporjo'. In *Shilpi Shilpo o Samaj*. Kolkata: Anustup Prakashani: 73–103.

Som, Sovon. 1992. 'The Art of Jamini Roy and the Bengal Folk Paradigm'. In *Seminar Papers: Jamini Roy*. New Delhi: Lalit Kala Academi. 25–48.

Suhrawardy, Shahid. 1938. 'The Art of Jamini Roy'. In *Prefaces: Lectures on Art Subjects*. Calcutta: Calcutta University. 115–138.

Sunderason, Sanjukta. 2020. *Partisan Aesthetics: Modern Art and India's Long Decolonization*. Stanford: Stanford University Press.

Ukil, Satyasri. 2000. *Jamini Roy: The first but Forgotten Exhibition*. Mukul Dey Archives, reprinted from Art and Deal, May-June 2000. http://www.chitralekha.org/articles/jamini-roy/jamini-roy-first-forgotten-exhibition . Last accessed on 8.10.2020.

Vatsyayan, Kapila. Foreword to *Scroll Paintings of Bengal: Art in the Village*. Amitabh SenGupta Bloomington: Authorhouse. 5–8.

ACKNOWLEDGEMENTS

It was only because of the goodwill and generous help of numerous people that I could write this book during these troubled and uncertain times. Most of it was written during a period of total lockdown in Bengal when I had no access whatsoever to libraries, galleries or museums, and no travel was possible. Many people kindly sent me scanned copies of books, articles, even archival material, among whom I am most indebted to Debashis Ghosh from Bangalore, a discerning art collector, who literally sent me hundreds of scanned pages of very old documents lying in his collection as well as images of some of Jamini Roy's rare paintings. Indranath Majumdar, likewise, extended invaluable help by way of procuring documents. These would have been difficult for me to procure even in the best of times. I am deeply grateful to Reena Lath of Akar Prakar Gallery for allowing me to have images from their Gallery collection as well as the collection of Mukund Lath, and to Richa Agarwal of Emami Art for responding immediately to my request and sharing images of the entire Jamini

Roy collection of Emami. Likewise, Sikha Roy of Birla Academy helped me to procure images from the Birla Academy collection—I am grateful to Mrs Jayshree Mohta for allowing me to have these. Vikram Bachhawat of Aakriti Art Gallery—a dear friend without whom my art writing would not have begun—also helped me by providing images from his own collection. Cory Woodall, assistant curator of San Diego Museum of Art, made sure I received images of three Roy paintings in their collection as soon as the Museum reopened after a prolonged period of closure due to the pandemic. Ganesh Pratap Singh's help had been invaluable, and I would remain forever grateful for the way he fished out images of Jamini Roy's very old photographs from his impressive and immense collection, even in the middle of a very busy schedule. Debabrata Roy, the artist's grandson, had spoken to me for hours, sharing significant anecdotes about his grandfather, and also shared the valuable photograph of Roy with Rabindranath Tagore. Prasanta Daw, likewise, had enriched me with his experiences, and also Sanjit Chowdhury, who helped me to make new and meaningful connections that proved enormously significant for my work. Jogen Chowdhury, always supportive of my efforts, had continuously encouraged me with his kind words, especially when the times were dark and bleak. I am also thankful to Nirmal Kanti Bhattacharjee, the Director of Niyogi Books, for his trust in me.

Many of the books I needed could be found in the collection of my father, Saktibrata Ghosh, who had left us many years ago yet continues to touch my life in unimaginable ways, as does my departed mother, Namita Ghosh. Samindranath Majumdar's impressive collection of art books took care of the rest; to him I remain forever grateful for the unconditional help he extended for my work, sharing insights, finding leads for rare images and documents, and generally for being there for me with those strong positive vibes for which he is known. My son Aaranyak, matured beyond his years mainly due to the pandemic, allowed me the space I needed and took care of his studies alone. I am also deeply grateful to my forever friends—Arpita Sen, Shakuntala Ghosh and Sharmila Chakraborty—for encouraging me each step of the way.

Many people came forward to make this book possible. If I have missed naming any of them inadvertently, the fault is entirely mine.

JAMINI ROY: HIS ART AND LIFE

(01) Untitled. *Pen and ink on paper. 8 x 13 inch. Courtesy: Akar Prakar*

(02) Boatmen. *Oil on canvas. 15.5 x 17.5 inch. Courtesy: Akar Prakar*

(03) Krishna and Balaram. *Gouache on paper. 5.5 x 18.5 inch. Courtesy: Akar Prakar*

(04) Cat. *Gouache on paper. 9.5 x 13 inch. Courtesy: Akar Prakar*

(05) Untitled. *3.25 x 4.75 inch. Courtesy: Akar Prakar*

(06) Untitled. *Pen and ink on paper. 5 x 5.25 inch. Courtesy: Akar Prakar*

(07) Mary and Jesus with Four Apostles. *Pen and ink on paper. 4.5 x 7 inch. Courtesy: Akar Prakar*

(08) Untitled. *Tempera on board. 4.25 x 5.5 inch. Courtesy: Akar Prakar*

(09) Cat and Fish-1. *Gouache on paper. 11.00 x 16.50 inch. Courtesy: Emami Art*

(10) Mary and Jesus. *Gouache on paper. 36.5 x 21.5 inch. Courtesy: Akar Prakar*

(11) Naika from Kalighat. *Ink & wash on paper. 23.75 x 15 inch. Courtesy: Akar Prakar*

(12) Elephant Rider. *Gouache on paper. 17.50 x 13.50 inch. Courtesy: Emami Art*

(13) Horse. *Tempera on card-board. 14.00 x 12.00 inch. Courtesy: Emami Art*

(14) Ganesh-Janani. *Water Colour. 32 x 47 cm. Courtesy: Birla Academy of Art and Culture.*

(15) Landscape. *Tempera on paper. 43 x 31 cm. Courtesy: Birla Academy of Art and Culture.*

(16) Gopini. *Water Colour. 75 x 60 cm. Courtesy: Birla Academy of Art and Culture.*

(17) Grand Mother. *Pastel. 27 x 45 cm. Courtesy: Birla Academy of Art and Culture.*

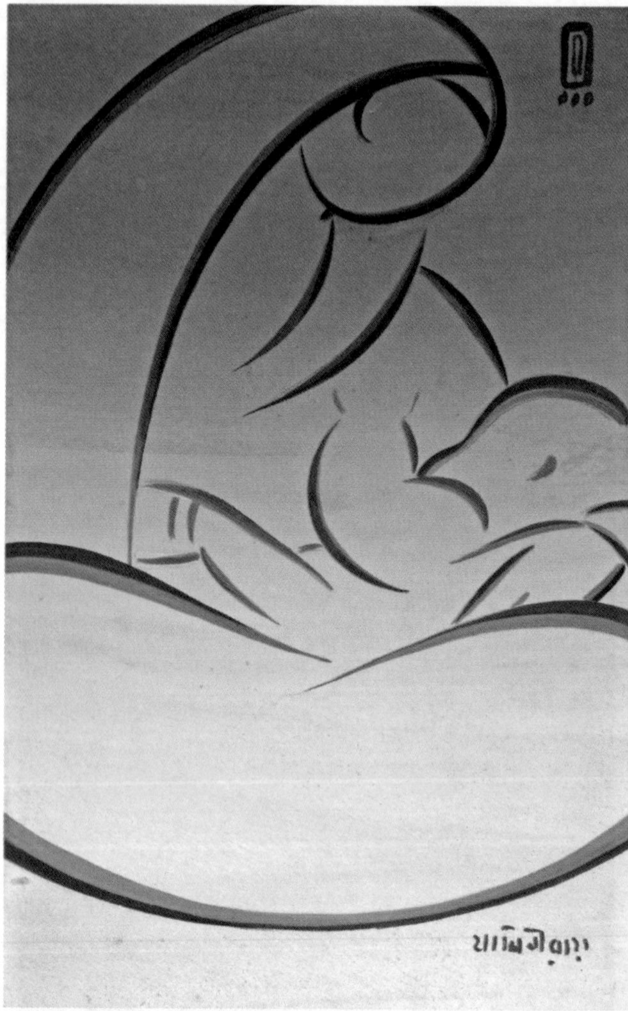

(18) Mother and Child. Tempera. *26.5 x 41 cm. Courtesy: Birla Academy of Art and Culture.*

(19) Jesus Christ, Crucifixion. *Oil on cloth. 27.00 x 18.50 inches. Courtesy: Emami Art*

(20) Ravana and Sita. *Gouache on paper. 13.50 x 17.50 inch. Courtesy: Birla Academy of Art and Culture.*

(21) Manasa, the Snake Goddess. *Gouache. 34.2 x 52 cm. Courtesy: San Diego Museum of Art*

(22) Untitled. *Tempera on board. 13 x 17 inch.*
Courtesy: Aakriti Art Gallery

(23) Agnipareeksha. *Tempera on board. 15.5 x 13.0 inch.*
Courtesy: Aakriti Art Gallery

(24) Untitled. *Drawing on paper. 6.5 x 4.0 inch.*
Courtesy: Aakriti Art Gallery

Roy in his studio. Photo courtesy: Ganesh Pratap Singh

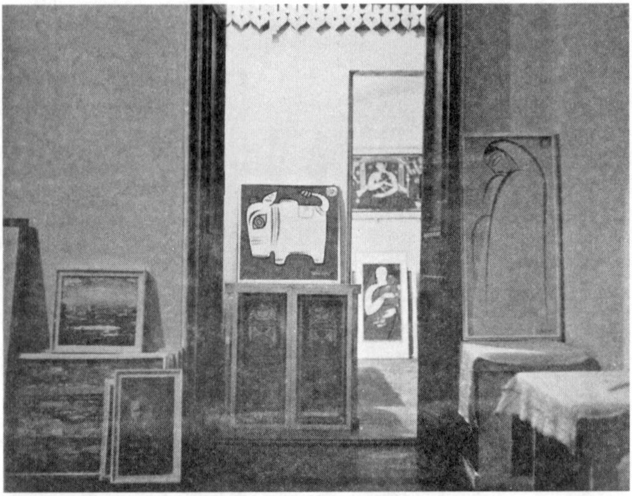

Roy's studio. Photo courtesy: Ganesh Pratap Singh

Roy in conversation. Photo courtesy: Ganesh Pratap Singh

Roy with Tagore. Photo courtesy: Debabrata Roy

Paintings on display at Roy's studio. Photo courtesy: Ganesh Pratap Singh

Roy's painting on pottery. Photo courtesy: Ganesh Pratap Singh